# MAGNA CARTA UNRAVELLED

*The Case for Christian Freedoms Today*

# MAGNA CARTA UNRAVELLED

*The Case for Christian Freedoms Today*

Wilberforce Publications

First published in Great Britain in 2015 by
Wilberforce Publications Limited
70 Wimpole Street, London W1G 8AX

## ISBN 978-0-957572-54-6

Printed by Imprint Digital, Exeter

# Contents

FOREWORD – The Baroness Cox     9
BIOGRAPHIES     11
INTRODUCTION – The Rev. Lynda Rose     17

Chapter 1: The Rev. Lynda Rose     25
THE RELEVANCE OF MAGNA CARTA TODAY
*1.1 Rights – Myth or Reality*
*1.2 Secularism*
*1.3 Origins and Spread of Secularism*
*1.4 Competing Religions: Islam*
*1.5 What would the UK look like if we became*
*an Islamic State?*
*1.6 Society at a Crossroads*
*1.7 Defending Christian 'Rights'*
*1.8 Time to Mobilise*
Endnotes

Chapter 2: Philip Quenby     49
THE CASE FOR CHRISTIAN FREEDOMS:
AN HISTORICAL PERSPECTIVE
*2.1 Introduction*
*2.2 Freedom*
*2.3 Democracy*
*2.4 Rule of Law*
*2.5 Consequences*
*2.6 Conclusion*
Endnotes

Chapter 3: Bishop Michael Nazir-Ali     69
MAGNA CARTA: BACKGROUND AND
FOREGROUND
*3.1 Introduction*
*3.2 The Background*
*3.3 The Church and Magna Carta*
*3.4 The Foreground*
*3.5 How Magna Carta Challenges us Today*

**Chapter 4: Professor Roger Trigg**     79
**THE CENTRALITY OF RELIGIOUS FREEDOM**
*4.1 Magna Carta*
*4.2 Why is Religious Freedom Important?*
*4.3 Religious Freedom in a Secular Society*
*4.4 Is Religious Freedom Special?*
*4.5 The Limits of Manifestation of Religion*
Endnotes

**Chapter 5: John Scriven**     105
**FREEDOM AND THE STATE**
*5.1 Introduction*
*5.2 Free Will and Reason*
*5.3 Determinism and Utopianism*
*5.4 Human Imperfection and Government*
*5.5 Personal Responsibility*
*5.6 Freedom of Belief and the State*
*5.7 The Power of the State and Magna Carta*
*5.8 Freedom and the State in Education*
*5.9 Problems with Human Rights*
*5.10 Equality and Diversity*
*5.11 The Equality Act 2010*
*5.12 Freedom of Expression and the Law*
*5.13 Cases on Freedom, and 'Reasonable Accommodation'*
*5.14 Conclusion*
Endnotes

**Chapter 6: The Baroness Cox**     129
**THE APPLICATION OF SHARIA LAW IN THE UK**
*6.1 Introduction*
*6.2 The Problem of 'Courts' that are not Courts*
*6.3 The Problem of Intimidation*
*6.4 The Problem of 'Marriages' that are not Marriages*
*6.5 Testimonies*
*6.6 Conclusion*
Endnotes

**Chapter 7: Robert S. Harris**                     145
**EXERCISING RELIGIOUS BELIEF AND**
**CONSCIENCE IN TWENTY-FIRST CENTURY**
**BRITAIN**
*7.1 Objectives*
*7.2 Preliminary Considerations*
*7.3 Public vs Private*
*7.4 Pluralism*
*7.5 Tolerance*
*7.6 Human Rights in Context*
*7.7 Article 9 (2): Questions of Limits*
*7.8 Tyranny of the Presumed Majority*
*7.9 Secularism and the Drive to Alienate Christianity*
*7.10 Exercising Belief and Conscience in the Workplace*
*7.11 Lord Carey's Intervention*
*7.12 The UK Government Submission and*
*Strasbourg Judgments*
*7.13 Conscientious Objection to Abortion*
*7.14 Questions of Accommodation*
*7.15 Seeing Beyond 'The Problems'*
Endnotes

**Chapter 8: Paul Diamond**                     187
**THE CLASH OF MORALITIES:**
**PERSONAL REFLECTION AND THE LAW**
**OF RELIGIOUS LIBERTY**
*8.1 Introduction*
*8.2 A Personal Indulgence*
*8.3 Background*
*8.4 Harry Hammond – The Last English Martyr?*
*8.5 The Offence of the Cross*
*8.6 The War on Christian Conscience and Morals*
*8.7 Not So Special Sunday*
*8.8 The Turn Around: 2013*
*8.9 Religious Free Speech: Compositing Articles 9 and 10*
*8.10 Conclusion*
Endnotes

# FOREWORD

## The Baroness Cox

On 15th June 1215, with the country on the brink of civil war, King John met with the barons at Runnymede. What transpired was, in effect, the conclusion of a peace treaty, with John guaranteeing to uphold the freedoms of the Church and to govern according to the law; and the barons, for their part, re-swearing their allegiance. The document in which these undertakings were spelt out and to which John affixed his seal was the Magna Carta.

Today this Charter is rightly viewed as one of the most famous documents in the world, protecting the rights of the individual against the coercive use of power by the State, and laying the foundations for democracy worldwide. But what is the reality of these protections today?

Across the Western world, and especially in the UK, much is made of Human Rights, in particular the rights to freedom of speech and of belief. We regard them as being so much a part of our society as to be automatic! Yet increasingly we are seeing restrictions being placed upon these ancient freedoms.

The global threat of terrorism has rightly seen increased measures designed to prevent the spread of Islamic fundamentalism and stop radicalization by what are termed 'hate preachers'. But new legislation restructuring the moral frame of society is also resulting in increased control over what people may and may not say more generally, to the extent that established doctrines of Christian faith conflicting with moral redefinition are now being branded hate speech and discrimination, with severe penalties being imposed on those who express them in public. In such a climate, freedom of speech functions only within carefully defined limits, and thus appears increasingly under threat.

The collected essays in this book are the result of a conference commemorating the 800th anniversary of Magna Carta. They look at the historical foundations for the protection of our freedoms, and from that point examine and analyse the changing face of human rights law in the UK today; in particular, the challenges presented to what have traditionally been regarded as our fundamental freedoms.

I warmly commend this book to all people concerned with issues surrounding freedom of speech and freedom of belief; to legal practitioners practising in the field of human rights; and to the law-makers of this land, whose responsibility is to pass laws that will protect and uphold our society, safeguarding the democratic freedoms that underpin our country in ways that will ensure justice and fairness for all and pass on these freedoms, which we have inherited, to our children and our grandchildren – undiminished.

# BIOGRAPHIES

*The Rev. Lynda Rose*

Lynda Rose is an Anglican priest and writer. Originally called to the Bar, she subsequently felt called to ministry and was amongst the first women to be ordained in the UK. She served for a number of years in parish ministry in and around Oxford, but more recently has devoted her energies to campaigning on pro-life and related Christian issues. She is CEO of *Voice for Justice UK*, and also serves as Joint Convenor of the *House of Lords and Commons Family and Child Protection Group*. She is author of several books for both the religious and general markets.

*Philip Quenby*

Philip Quenby was born in Nottingham in 1961, and educated at Nottingham High School and *Queens' College, Cambridge*. He is writer and presenter of the forthcoming five-part television documentary *Magna Carta Unlocked*, which traces the influence of Magna Carta in politics, science, society, law and warfare. His publications include *Redeeming a Nation* (Onwards and Upwards Publishers, 2011) and *Moses and Pharaoh* (Onwards and Upwards Publishers, 2014).

### Bishop Michael Nazir-Ali

For 15 years Bishop Michael served as the 106th Bishop of Rochester. Originally from Pakistan, he was the first non-white Diocesan Bishop in the Church of England, appointed in 1994. Before that he was the General Secretary of the *Church Mission Society* (CMS) from 1989-1994, and before that Bishop of Raiwind in Pakistan. In 1999 he became a member of the House of Lords where he has been active in a number of areas of national and international concern. He is now President of the *Oxford Centre for Training, Research, Advocacy and Dialogue* (OXTRAD). Bishop Michael has been a visiting lecturer in a number of universities and colleges in the UK, Canada, the USA and Australia. He is the author of eleven books and countless articles on Faith and Public Life, Freedom of Belief, Bioethics, Mission, Ecumenism, the Anglican Communion, and relations with people of other faiths (particularly Islam). In 2005, he was awarded the *Paul Harris Fellowship* by *Rotary International*.

### Professor Roger Trigg

Roger Trigg is Emeritus Professor of Philosophy at the *University of Warwick*. From 2007-11 he was co-Director of a project, jointly with the Faculty of Anthropology, on the cognitive science of religion, based in the Ian Ramsey Centre, University of Oxford. In 2006-7 he was Interim Director of the Centre. He was Founding President of the *British Society for the Philosophy of Religion* (1993-6), and more recently President of the *European Society for Philosophy of Religion* (2008-10). He was the first President of the *British Philosophical Association* in 2003-4, having chaired its predecessor, the *National Committee for Philosophy*. He is the joint editor, with Wentzel van Huyssteen of Princeton, of an international series of monographs on science and religion, and the author of many books on philosophy. He is a Senior Research Fellow at the *Ian Ramsey Centre for Science and Religion* and has been until recently an Associate Scholar of the *Religious Freedom Project* at the Berkley Center, *Georgetown University*, Washington D.C. His most recent publications include *Equality, Freedom and Religion* (Oxford University Press, 2012) and *Religious Diversity: Philosophical and Political Dimensions* (Cambridge University Press, 2014).

### John Scriven

John Scriven is a graduate of *Trinity College, Cambridge* and has been a commercial lawyer with an international law firm for over thirty years. He is the author of *A Contractual Guide to Major Construction Projects* (Sweet & Maxwell, 1999) and *EPC Contracts and Major Projects* (Sweet & Maxwell, 2012), and is a visiting lecturer at *Reading University*. He was Chairman of *The Lawyers' Christian Fellowship* from 2003 to 2011. He contributed to *Religion and Law* (Theos, 2012) and is the author of *Belief and the Nation* (Wilberforce Publications, 2013).

### The Baroness Cox

Baroness Cox was created a Life Peer in 1982 for her contributions to education and has served as a Deputy Speaker of the House of Lords from 1985 to 2005. Baroness Cox now sits in the House of Lords as a crossbencher and is a frequent contributor to Lords debates on people suffering oppression and persecution, including those in Sudan, South Sudan, Nigeria, and Burma. Baroness Cox's humanitarian aid work has taken her on many missions to conflict zones, such as the historically Armenian land of Nagorno-Karabakh, Sudan, Nigeria, Uganda, Burma and Indonesia as well as to other troubled countries such as North Korea. In recognition of her work in the international humanitarian and human rights arenas, she has been awarded the *Commander Cross of the Order of Merit of the Republic of Poland*; the prestigious *Wilberforce Award*; the *International Mother Teresa Award* from the All India Christian Council; the *Mkhitar Gosh Medal* conferred by the President of the Republic of Armenia; and the anniversary medal presented by Lech Walesa, the former President of Poland, at the 25th anniversary of the Polish Solidarity Movement. Baroness Cox has also been awarded an *Honorary Fellowship of the Royal College of Surgeons of England* and Honorary Doctorates by universities in the United Kingdom, the United States of America, the Russian Federation and Armenia.

### Robert S. Harris

Robert S. Harris serves as the Joint Convenor of the *Lords and Commons Family and Child Protection Group*, in which he has been active since 2011. He co-edited the Group's report, *Stolen Childhood: Contemporary Issues of Family Breakdown*. He is the author of *Is There a Case for Same-Sex Marriage? Questions of Eligibility and Consequences* (2012), commended by Lord Mackay of Clashfern (former Lord Chancellor), Parliamentarians and senior Church leaders. He has spoken at a number of parliamentary events and in 2012 organised a parliamentary conference dealing with the sexualisation of children. In his role as Director of *Voice for Justice UK* he organised a conference on religious liberty in 2015 that led to the publication of *Magna Carta Unravelled*. He wrote a Briefing Paper on issues of sexuality and the Christian faith which was submitted to the *Pilling Commission on Human Sexuality* (2012). Robert read Philosophy at *University College London* and holds a Graduate Diploma in Law from the *College of Law*.

## *Paul Diamond, LL.M.*

Paul Diamond is a leading barrister in the law of religious liberty, combining his considerable strength in this field with his knowledge of public and European law. He is an expert in European human rights law, EU law and certain aspects of international law. As Standing Counsel to the *Christian Legal Centre* he specializes in bringing difficult cases to the attention of the British public. His cases include the right to wear a Cross by a British Airways member of staff, the right for Christians to foster children, the right of a nurse and doctor to pray for patients, and many more. He has written numerous articles for legal journals, including an academic article endorsed by Lord Denning on European law. Paul has appeared at all levels of the court system including the *House of Lords* and the *European Court of Human Rights*.

# INTRODUCTION

## The Rev. Lynda Rose

The United Kingdom is at a crossroads, with the soul of our nation at stake.

Even fifty years ago, the notion of a conference addressing Christian freedoms would have seemed slightly absurd. After all, we were a Christian country, so all of our freedoms, by definition, would have been "Christian", surely? But fast-forward a few decades, and that picture has changed. Notionally, the UK remains Christian. At the time of writing the Anglican Church is still the Established Church of England and, according to the 2011 census for England and Wales, 59.3% of the population still self-identify as Christian. Yet today we have been overtaken by multiculturalism, with its plethora of non-integrated belief systems. At the same time, and counterpointed against this, we have a highly vociferous secular lobby, campaigning vigorously for exclusion from the public arena of anything and everything that even hints at religion.

The result is that, even though our society and culture are founded on Judaeo-Christian values and ideas, Christians have found themselves increasingly marginalised, portrayed in the media as prehistoric fossils with views that are not just calcified, but dangerous. More bizarrely, the religion and belief systems of non-Christians, even where violent and advancing values in conflict with those of the UK, appear protected and treated with respect, with their rights prioritised over those holding to the established Church.

The truth is that we are seeing the ruthless imposition of a new value system that is at odds with our Judaeo-Christian heritage and which, though holding itself out as 'neutral', is in reality a new and competing religion, striving for supremacy. The language and culture of Rights may have become sacrosanct in Western culture, but in practice today 'rights' are very selectively applied, and are increasingly being used as a weapon against anything that criticizes or contravenes the new value system.

Democracy itself is being manipulated through highly vocal campaigns in the media to overturn and suppress the very values on which our nation was founded, the origins of which are clearly evident in Magna Carta.

It is against this background that the idea for a conference and book commemorating the 800th anniversary of this important and highly influential document was conceived. Today, throughout the world, Magna Carta – sealed at Runnymede on June 15th, 1215 – has iconic status, seen as a hallmark for the rule of law and for democracy. Essentially, it was a peace treaty between King John and the rebel barons, who were in open conflict following John's maladministration and abuse of power. Making the king equally subject to the law, and providing protection against the coercive use of power by the State, it became over time foundational for protection of the rights of the common man, the cornerstone of English liberties. Its influence has spread throughout the world.

It is now apparent, however, that though the assertion of rights has become almost a mantra for justifying any and every conceivable behaviour, Christian rights are increasingly seen as falling into a different category, and so the conference evolved into an examination and defence of

Christian freedoms in 21st century Britain. The resulting book is a collection of essays ranging from an examination of the origins of Magna Carta and its application, development and scope through history, to the situation now prevailing in 21st century Britain.

The book is divided into eight chapters, six of which are expanded versions of the talks given at conference, but with two essential additions, the first from lawyer and historian, Philip Quenby, and the second from Baroness Caroline Cox. The whole starts with an overview chapter from myself, arguing that Human Rights, far from being 'universal', are derived exclusively from the Judaeo-Christian concept that men and women are worthy of honour and respect by virtue of their humanity as made in the image of God. The three-stranded battle between secularism, Islam, and Christianity, currently gripping society, therefore becomes explicable as a battle between competing belief systems, which it is necessary to understand if we are to have any hope of maintaining Christian belief. Starting from this basis, the book then examines in detail the history and origins of rights, before moving on to address the growing restrictions on Human and Christian freedoms increasingly evident in society today.

The historical background to the evolution of democracy and the rule of law, grounded in Magna Carta, is provided by Philip Quenby. Starting from the position that history, values and culture are all interlinked, he argues that we need to see and understand our past in order to understand the way ahead, clearly showing how biblical teaching has been foundational to the development of English law and democracy. Going back to Saxon law, he delineates the debt owed by society to the Bible and Christian teaching, showing how the liberties and moral freedoms today associated with Magna Carta developed from the faith of those who stood against tyranny and for freedom. In particular, Philip shows how biblical teaching has been foundational to the development of democracy and English law, in marked contrast to continental systems derived from the traditions of Roman law, to which the same limits on executive power did not apply.

Bishop Michael Nazir-Ali continues and expands this theme from a more specifically theological position, exploring the Christian basis of the early Anglo-Saxon law codes and of Magna Carta. With their explicit acknowledgment of 'a higher law' to which all are equally subject, Bishop Michael explores the moral and spiritual impact of the Judaeo-Christian tradition on the nation today, concluding that the Christian tradition remains vital for the moral and spiritual welfare of the people, in terms both of policy and of legislation.

Developing this view, philosopher Professor Roger Trigg addresses the vital question of the reality and importance of religious freedom. For there to be genuine freedom for the individual, he argues, there needs first to be freedom for institutions that remain separate from the State. Otherwise the individual is reduced to being merely a creature of the State, and true freedom becomes impossible. He emphasizes that Magna Carta locates the State firmly under divine authority, reinforcing the fact that the State should never regard itself as the ultimate authority. In a masterly analysis, Professor Trigg examines the challenges posed by the rise of secularism, arguing that protection from arbitrary rule and the unbridled use of power starts, and can only start, with freedom of religion.

Starting from a different viewpoint, lawyer and philosopher John Scriven reflects on the nature and importance of freedom, putting the case that freedom is grounded in the created order and a part of the purposes of

God. In light of that he then analyses both the concept of free will, and some of the secular challenges to freedom, impressively refuting the idea that morality is a matter of choice. Examining the validity and functions of the State, he concludes that Christian values both reflect and maintain the order and purposes of God and are therefore indispensable to the maintenance of the freedom that gives true respect to the individual.

Having analysed the basis and origins of rights, the book then moves to an examination of the situation today, beginning with the chapter by Baroness Caroline Cox, who was our Conference Chairman and is a well-known campaigner against injustice worldwide. Currently working to help abused women from ethnic communities, she describes in detail the covert but relentless spread and influence of Sharia law in the UK. In particular, she highlights points of conflict between the application of English and Sharia law, perhaps most clearly seen in the many injustices to women. Pointing out that marriage under Sharia law in the UK rarely carries the status of civil marriage, she shows how Muslim women are not only vulnerable to abuse but also, if divorced by their husbands, are left entirely without redress or protection. Under the cloak of multiculturalism, she says, this growing evil – which runs contrary to our heritage – is being systemically ignored, with the result that women are not just suffering but being deprived of their rights. To ensure justice for these voiceless women and others, therefore, we need rigorously to enforce the rule of law, which is unacceptably undermined by allowing the application of Sharia.

Christian rights campaigner and activist Robert S. Harris follows this with an important analysis of the growing restrictions being placed on the manifestation of Christian belief and practice within society, clearly showing the incompatibilities that result from the imposition of 'tolerance, pluralism and diversity' called for by the new liberal and secular value system. Examining the meaning of these terms within the context of human rights, he analyses their application and interpretation as seen in four cases: Nadia Eweida (not allowed to wear a cross at work); Lillian Ladele (the Christian Registrar who objected on conscientious grounds to being required to preside at civil partnerships); sex counsellor Gary Macfarlane (dismissed for gross misconduct by Relate, after expressing reservation about providing sex therapy to same-sex couples); and the right of conscientious objection to abortion raised by the case of the two Scottish midwives Mary Doogan and Concepta Wood. Identifying 'religious illiteracy' as a major problem, he concludes that the demands of political correctness pose a clear and present danger to the fundamental freedoms of conscience, belief, and expression, which can be remedied only by legislative support and a clear education policy that unequivocally supports religious freedom.

Notwithstanding the growing number of cases, many today still try and maintain that concerns over freedom of speech and belief are grossly exaggerated, and that allegations of increasing Christian marginalisation are not just over-hyped, but untrue. Our final chapter, by Human Rights' barrister Paul Diamond, talking about some of the many cases he has been involved in, shows clearly that, far from being overstated, the reality of discrimination against Christians is chillingly real. Going back to the relative innocence of 1988, when he was appointed barrister to the Keep Sunday Special Campaign, Paul traces the creeping climate of discrimination – from the case of Harry Hammond, assaulted for preaching against homosexuality on the street, then himself arrested for having incited the offence, to the latest cases clearly favouring the prioritisation of LGBT and Muslim rights over Christian rights of conscience and belief. He concludes that there is undeniable evidence of growing hostility towards the Christian faith, seen not just in the courts, but in society at large.

Magna Carta Unravelled is intended as a wake-up call. If we now fail to defend the Judaeo-Christian heritage that underpins our nation and has given rise to the values we hold dear, we shall lose them. Worse, we shall see the imposition of a totalitarian and repressive value system that allows only those 'freedoms' that support its continuance. The rebranding of morality and increased restrictions on freedom of expression and conscience that result, far from increasing our freedoms, will make us all puppets of the State.

No doubt many people, having lived in a period of relative peace and freedom after the defeat of Nazism and the demise of the Soviet Union, will regard this as unduly alarmist. Yet the history of the twentieth and early twenty-first centuries makes clear that our civilisation is constantly under threat, and a reminder of the underpinnings of that civilisation is essential if it – and all of us – are to continue to enjoy the hard won freedoms that come exclusively from our Judaeo-Christian heritage.

Chapter One

# THE RELEVANCE OF MAGNA CARTA TODAY

The Rev. Lynda Rose

## 1.1 RIGHTS – MYTH OR REALITY?

According to the United Nations, human rights are 'rights inherent to all human beings, whatever our nationality, place of residence, sex, national or ethnic origin, colour, religion, language, or any other status. We are all equally entitled to our human rights without discrimination. These rights are … interdependent and indivisible.'[1] In its Universal Declaration of Human Rights, which it calls a Magna Carta for all humanity,[2] the UN spells out these rights as including freedom of belief and religion, the right to life, the right to be treated equally before the law, the right to freedom without imprisonment for just cause, the right to marry and have a family, the right to education and so on. The wording says explicitly that these 'rights' are inherent to the human condition – effectively entitlements written in stone, and therefore not open to question by any rational, educated man or woman. But is this really so?

Magna Carta is one of the most celebrated and influential documents in history, the foundation not just of British democracy, but of democratic aspiration worldwide. William Pitt the Elder called it 'the bible of the English constitution', while Lord Denning, former Master of the Rolls, said it was 'The greatest constitutional document of all times – the foundation of the freedom of the individual against the arbitrary authority of the despot.' Franklin Roosevelt in 1941, in a speech defending democracy and freedom under the shadow of war, said:

*'The democratic aspiration is no mere recent phase in human history. It is human history. It permeated the ancient life of early peoples. It blazed anew in the Middle Ages. It was written in Magna Carta'.*[3]

However, this foundational Charter didn't stand on 'rights'. Rather, it set out 'liberties' claimed by the barons in face of the abusive and coercive use of power by the king, who had radically overstepped the mark. This distinction is important because, while it may seem pedantic, 'rights' implies innate entitlement or privilege, while 'liberties' are more correctly defined as a right or privilege *enjoyed by prescription or grant* (as defined in The Oxford Dictionary). In the event, Magna Carta was a peace treaty between warring factions – the barons and John – and it made the king subject to the law.

At the time, this was revolutionary. In England, by custom and tradition laid down by the Anglo-Saxons, the role of the king was to care for and lead the people, *under God*. The king himself was regarded as subject to God and therefore under His rule. The sovereign had responsibility, so that the government of the country functioned by way of mutual and reciprocal obligation between the king and the people. With the coming of the Normans, however, this approach changed. Certainly William the Conqueror invoked God and claimed divine justification for his rule – you couldn't really be a king without that in those days – but in terms of actual government, God didn't get much of a look in. William's laws at heart were secular, and the culturally required Christian reference that prefixed all laws was included strictly for the purposes of legitimisation. The Church was kept under tight rein.

John, an autocrat with a total absence of sensitivity, took this to new and unprecedented heights. In his quest for money, he rode roughshod over any and all rights of the barons, imprisoning without trial, abusing inheritance provisions, and imposing swingeing fines as a way of levying tax. Unsurprising then that the barons rebelled, holding up as a model the rose-tinted age of King Alfred, when the land was justly and rightly governed, and everyone lived happy and prosperous lives! Runnymede was the outcome of a long and bitter struggle.

Magna Carta went back to the legal code of Alfred the Great, in itself based on three earlier Saxon codes, but to which Alfred had prefixed the Ten Commandments, i.e. he had explicitly based the law of the land on the law of God. This had become the foundation for the common law of England, and it was this that subsequently served as the foundation for Magna Carta.

But, to revert to the question of whether rights are inherent – elsewhere in the world, both historically and geographically, very different values have prevailed. The Aztecs, for example, believed the gods (and they had a fair number) had to be fed by human blood – both to win their favour, and to keep them strong, which was the only thing that would ensure the survival of the universe. As a result they went in for human sacrifice, and any arguments about respect for the individual and the right to life would have had zero impact. They also practised slavery, as did most peoples in the ancient world. But at the same time they had compulsory education for all children – which they did see as a 'right', and which is amazing when you think about it. In England we had to wait until 1870, and even then it was only compulsory between the ages of 5-10.

Or look at the Romans. They were one of the most successful empires there has ever been, and actually highly religious. As the American theologian Rodney Stark has pointed out, everything – every meeting, every decision, every act – was accompanied by a religious ceremony. But their primary value was allegiance to, and wellbeing of, the State, and individuals had value only in so much as they were a part of that State. So, whatever rights the individual had came not from any qualities or value inherent to them personally – the human condition – but from their inclusion in and contribution to the State.[4] A good example of what this meant in practice is seen in the Apostle Paul, who in Caesarea claimed the right to trial before the Emperor – not because of any idea of justice that allowed the right of appeal to a higher court, but simply because he was a Roman citizen.[5]

The point to be made is that, at any one time, the values held by a society reflect the predominant beliefs and practice of the individuals who comprise that society. And historically most societies have been rooted not in the notion of respect for the individual (and, by extension, of entitlement) but in compliance and obligation; often in fact, by subjugation. So the language of rights, based on respect for the individual, is something very specific to Western culture and, whatever the secularists try and maintain, it is beyond any doubt that this comes directly from our Judaeo-Christian heritage, and is based on the idea of respect for the individual as made in the image of God, spelt out from the very beginning of Scripture:

*Then God said, 'Let us make mankind in our image, in our likeness, so that they may rule over the fish in the sea and the birds in the sky, over the livestock and all the wild animals, and over all the creatures that move along the ground' (NIV).[6]*

Until fairly recently, this understanding was framed in terms not of rights, but of responsibilities. Men and women were created to rule over and care for the earth but, as laid down in the Gospel of Luke, "From everyone who has been given much, much will be demanded: and from the one who has been entrusted with much, much more will be demanded" (NIV).[7]

From around the middle of the last century, however, there began a shift in perspective, so that increasingly our responsibilities became viewed as inalienable rights; not what we owed to society, but what society owed to us. Whichever view you favour, however, the idea that men and women are intrinsically worthy of respect comes from a Judaeo-Christian worldview. In no other society or culture of the world has the individual, simply by virtue of his or her humanity, ever been accorded the same value or respect.

This matters because what we need to recognise today is that we are in the middle of a predominantly three-stranded ideological war: between Christianity, secularism, and Islam. Now at first glance it may appear that 'secularism' is the independent referee in a struggle between competing religions – but this is not true. Secularism does not start from a position of neutrality. Secularism is also a faith system, in reality a religion, with its own gods and aspirations, and at the current time it is battling for supremacy. In order to undermine traditional religious, and especially Christian, influence on society and marginalise believers, it will use and exploit every tool at its disposal. This, perhaps short-sightedly (and some might feel rather astonishingly), includes the exploitation of Islam, promoted as of equal standing with Christianity in order to downgrade the status of the UK as a Christian country. This is a risky tactic, because Islam – more obviously a religion – is also battling for supremacy, most clearly seen in the drive to establish a global caliphate. The common factor shared by both these ideologies is that they identify Christianity and Judaism as the enemy – something to be not just suppressed but ultimately entirely eradicated.

## 1.2  SECULARISM

For secularists the apparent justification for their campaign is that over the centuries religion (and in particular Christianity) has been the cause of more violence, war, barbarity, torture and oppression than anything else on the planet.  In fact, the way they tell it, religion lies at the root of every evil under the sun, not least in the imposition of a repressive and damaging value system that runs contrary to nature and whose sole effect is to engender guilt.  They argue, therefore, that in these enlightened, scientific times such anachronistic superstition needs to be divested of influence and entirely removed from the public arena.

The website for the National Secular Society states:

*We campaign for a secular democracy with a separation of religion and state, where everyone's Human Rights are respected equally.*

*We work in the UK and Europe to challenge the disproportionate influence of religion on governments and in public life.  We provide a secular voice in the media, defending freedom and equality as a counterbalance to the powerful religious lobby and some of the more destructive religious impulses that can threaten human rights worldwide".*[8]

At first sight it might be said that this appears fairly innocuous; even reasonable, which, of course, is how the appeal is marketed to the public.  But unpack their agenda a little more carefully and you find a raft of measures designed to obliterate any and all trace of religious observance from the public arena.  Secularists appear to want religion to become a strictly under the counter activity!  They have campaigns, for example, to stop all public manifestation of worship;[9] to remove all religious observance and influence from schools and in medicine;[10] to remove public funding from Church schools – indeed, to close them altogether,[11] and to make illegal the mention of creationism and intelligent design in the teaching of science.[12]

The list goes on, but most bizarre – because it is so self-evidently contradictory – seems the secularists' claim to champion free speech. Under the banner 'freedom of expression', they boast that they robustly challenge religious "threats" to freedom of expression – but at the same time they claim to be campaigning vigorously against *all* attempts to restrict free speech or artistic expression. To those not versed in such niceties this may appear something of an oxymoron, but it would seem that for secularists freedom of speech has clearly defined limits. Apparently, we have the right and freedom to say and do absolutely anything we want … provided it doesn't support Christian morality or belief, in which case it's bigoted hate speech and must be stamped out.

## 1.3  THE ORIGINS AND SPREAD OF SECULARISM

This ideological battle for supremacy actually started around the second half of the nineteenth century with the birth of Marxism. If we are to have any chance of defending our faith and moral values today – our rights as Christians – then we must recognise and understand how this has happened. The task actually is not as easy as it sounds, because for the last 1500 years or so, we have tended to think that as Christians our position is unassailable. We are a Christian nation, the argument runs, with our laws founded upon and enshrined in the Bible. The rightness of our views is so self-evident that we don't need to defend them!

The truth is, when the threat first really emerged, with the Bolsheviks around a hundred years ago, the West simply didn't recognise what was going on. Certainly, we entirely failed to appreciate the challenge being made by the Russian Revolution, not just to monarchical forms of government and democracy, but to the very fabric of society. At the time the revolutionaries had confidently expected that their movement would catch fire and spread spontaneously across Europe, and into America. This, however, failed to happen so, to find out why, a Communist think-tank called the Institute for Social Research (I.S.R.), and comprised of Marxist intellectuals, was set up to investigate the reasons for the failure.

The group identified as the main problem the Judaeo-Christian legacy, which they saw as underpinning Western Society. Based on this analysis, and to pave the way for global Socialist revolution, they devised a complex psychological strategy aimed at bringing about complete destruction of the beliefs and institutions on which Western society rested, targeting specifically the family, which they saw as one of the main building blocks of society. It was a strategy designed to produce mass hopelessness and alienation, destroying faith in God and any idea of transcendent purpose that might provide some sort of unifying force for the common man. Rather too persuasively as it turned out, because Stalin, when he came to power, expelled the group for being too extreme. In 1924, forced to flee, they took refuge in Frankfurt, Germany, and so was born the infamous *Frankfurt School*.[13] In order to facilitate social psychosis and enable control, the group advocated such things as the teaching of sex and homosexuality to children; mass provision of contraceptives to school children; breakdown and destabilization of the family; promotion of mass immigration to destroy national identity; control and manipulation of the media; destabilization of the legal system; and dependency of all individuals on the State.[14]

It was a marriage of Marx and Freud – definitely not

made in heaven – and over the years has proved extremely successful, though not always popular. In 1933, following the rise to power of Hitler, the group was again expelled for being too dangerous, and ended up a couple of years later in America, where they continued to gain influence and develop their theories. What they came up with, in effect, was a manifesto for the creation of chaos in order to allow the imposition of totalitarian control.

Yet, even as late as 1969, when the Stonewall riots erupted in New York and the fight for gay rights began, the idea that the establishment and, by extension, Christianity might be under concentrated and sustained attack – through a carefully orchestrated strategy – would have seemed preposterous. Covertly, however, that was exactly what was going on. The Stonewall Inn was a notorious bar catering for gays, lesbians and transvestites in Greenwich Village. Described as "a street queen hangout in the heart of the ghetto",[15] unsurprisingly perhaps, it was run by the mafia. On 28th June 1969 a routine raid by the police unexpectedly provoked a week-long series of riots, as gays from all over the city flocked to protest. The New York Daily News carried the headline, "Homo Nest Raided, Queen Bees Are Stinging Mad".

In no attempt to pour oil on troubled waters, the article continued:

*She sat there with her legs crossed, the lashes of her mascara-coated eyes beating like the wings of a hummingbird. She was angry. She was so upset she hadn't bothered to shave. A day old stubble was beginning to push through the pancake makeup. She was a he. A queen of Christopher Street.*

*Last weekend the queens had turned commandos and stood bra strap to bra strap against an invasion of the helmeted Tactical Patrol Force. The elite police squad had*

*shut down one of their private gay clubs, the Stonewall Inn at*
*57 Christopher St., in the heart of a three-block homosexual*
*community in Greenwich Village. Queen Power reared its*
*bleached blonde head in revolt. New York City experienced*
*its first homosexual riot. "We may have lost the battle,*
*sweets, but the war is far from over," lisped an unofficial*
*lady-in-waiting from the court of the Queens.[16]*

It was to prove prophetic. Within days of the riots the gay community started discussing how to respond. The strategy was not finally fully articulated until 1989, when Marshall Kirk and Hunter Madsen brought out their groundbreaking and hugely influential book, *After the Ball: How America will Conquer Its Hatred and Fear of Gays in the '90s.*[17] Respectively, a Harvard educated neuropsychiatrist, and an expert on public persuasion tactics and social marketing, the pair laid out their strategy for the rebranding of morality, recasting gays as victims – where necessary rewriting history – with the aim of not just 'acceptance', but normalization. And, with that, the worm crawled out of the apple and into the heart of the establishment, so that the work of demolition from within began.

What ostensibly began as a movement to overcome prejudice has progressed far beyond that, becoming a drive – still continuing today – to push for the normalization of every imaginable perversion.[18] The conclusion is unavoidable that the Gay Liberation movement has been turned into a tool for something infinitely more sinister, very effectively implementing the strategies laid out by the Frankfurt School which, as we have seen, were aimed at the complete overthrow of Western society in order to pave the way for socialist revolution. The pace of change since that time has been truly startling.

It is, of course, not suggested that everyone who embraces secularist, humanist or LGBT ideas is signed up to the Frankfurt School, but this actually is the agenda that consciously or unconsciously they have been seduced into following. A constituency advocating one type of change has been used as a vehicle for more far-reaching social and cultural transformation, and there is no doubt that minority group interests have been ruthlessly exploited. Inevitably the value system that flows from this matrix of orchestrated destabilization reflects and reinforces the aspirations of this deeper, underlying ideology. So it's hardly surprising that freedom of speech is now being recast to demonise anything that implies criticism, permitting only comments that support the new *Weltanschauung*. Thus, as we have seen, anything beyond that is now recast as hate speech, whether it is the expression of personal opinion or a quotation from Scripture.

## 1.4  COMPETING RELIGIONS: ISLAM

We should counterpoint against this drive the rise of Islam, which is admittedly very different from secularism, but equally poses a threat to the traditional values of Europe and the West. One of the main Muslim complaints today is that Western society is corrupt – the Frankfurt School has done a good job. But it means Muslims are increasingly calling for social and legal recognition of their own values, not just within their own communities, but imposed on the wider society. Let us make no mistake, the growing dominance of Islam – even 'moderate' Islam – if allowed to progress unchecked, will ultimately involve the suppression and/or eradication of everything that runs contrary to their belief system, as set down in the Koran. This of course includes the suppression of Christianity – which we are already seeing violently enforced in other parts of the world where Islam is dominant. But it will also and at the same time radically change the whole face of Western society – overturning, in the process, those values currently being promoted by the secularists.

## 1.5  WHAT WOULD THE UK LOOK LIKE IF WE BECAME AN ISLAMIC STATE?

For a start, our financial system would have to change to make it Sharia compliant. This would be rapidly followed by a reconfiguration of our legal system, so as not to offend Muslim requirements. Then our academic systems would change to allow segregation, and women would be downgraded, subjected to dress codes and with restricted access to education; not allowed to drive, not allowed to talk to a man outside the family. If this were to happen, we might well then see arranged marriages becoming the norm, with women having little say.

All this may admittedly sound extreme in our currently tolerant and multicultural society, but it is a logical projection, supported by what we are already seeing in countries where Islam is the dominant belief system – countries such as, for example, Afghanistan, Saudi Arabia, Pakistan, Syria, Iran .... Of course Islamic countries differ in how rigorously they impose Koranic and traditional requirements – some indeed are struggling to maintain a more liberal and tolerant outlook. But we need to face up to the fact that the Koran does not allow divergent belief, on numerous occasions explicitly calling for the death of non-believers.[19] And, though moderate Muslims may assert that Islam is a religion of peace, the increasingly powerful radical wing that seems to be emerging worldwide seeks total dominance, calling for strict enforcement of the Koran, which includes the call for death to all unbelievers and apostates.

Inevitably, therefore, as radical influence spreads, we may well see factional violence erupting in the UK between competing Islamic groups. Should this happen, the balance of probability would surely give victory to the more ruthless militants, in which case the moderates might well find themselves suffering the same fate as other proscribed groups.

*"Our onslaught will not be a weak faltering affair. We shall fight as long as we live. We will fight until you turn to Islam, humbly seeking refuge. We will fight not caring whom we meet. We will fight whether we destroy ancient holdings or newly gotten gains. We have mutilated every opponent. We have driven them violently before us at the command of Allah and Islam. We will fight until our religion is established. And we will plunder them, for they must suffer disgrace"*: Ishaq: 58[20]

Actually, we are seeing the relentless creep of Islamisation in the UK already. David Cameron, for instance, has publicly supported the drive to make London a global hub for Islamic finance. When endorsing the launch of an Islamic index on the Stock Exchange in 2013, he reportedly said, "I want London to stand alongside Dubai as one of the great capitals of Islamic finance anywhere in the world".[21] What he didn't mention is that Islamic financial practice is wholly incompatible with Western banking. Under Islamic rules, for instance, you are not allowed to invest in gambling, pork, pornography, alcohol, or drugs. Similarly, a lender can't receive interest on loans – which means, for example, that, without a little financial trickery to bend the rules, mortgage providers can't offer a mortgage. So, to accommodate this, our mortgage lending rules have already been changed. In fact, the whole financial climate of this country is being incrementally restructured to make it Islam compliant.

In the same way, we're seeing a growing push to win acceptance of Sharia law. In 2009, the think tank Civitas found evidence of at least 85 Sharia courts operating across Britain,[22] while in March 2014 the Law Society issued guidelines on drafting sharia-compliant wills to be recognised by the English courts.[23] Although the Law Society was subsequently forced to back down and apologise, if these wills had gone ahead to become integrated into UK law, they would have penalised women and non-Muslims, and excluded all children born out of wedlock from inheritance.[24]

Despite this check, the slow creep of Muslim influence is progressing, with ever increasing numbers of British Muslims reportedly turning to traditional Islamic law (the Sharia courts) to settle disputes. But this is only part of a complex picture, because increasing numbers of reports also show Muslim vigilantes, often apparently converts, imposing extra judicial compliance with Sharia law on their local neighbourhoods.[25]

Such incidents may be swiftly dealt with and appear minor; but, should Sharia law gain wider traction, we may well find similar pressure being exerted for its broader acceptance and application, to the extent perhaps that it begins to override British law. Evidence of this already happening appeared in a recent story in The Telegraph, dated 17 February 2015. Under the headline, '*Grandfather's body could be exhumed after relatives of Muslim buried alongside complain he was an unbeliever*', it tells the story of a dispute centring on what is claimed to be the multi-faith Lychgate Lane Cemetery in Burbage, Leicestershire. An unnamed Muslim family apparently demanded the exhumation and burial elsewhere of an 89 year old Roman Catholic, Shadrack Smith, after he was buried in a plot adjacent to their relation, on the ground that it is forbidden for non-Muslims to be buried alongside Muslims. In the UK, still nominally a Christian country, the complaint beggars belief, but what is really astounding is that Burbage Borough Council appear to have supported the demand, warning Mr Smith's family that his body may have to be moved.[26]

In such a situation, whose 'rights' prevail? Those of Christianity (the belief system which forms the basis of our culture), or those of Islam (the notoriously intolerant newcomers)? Does it matter? Or should we just accept that we will only be offered Halal meals on flights, and that all meat displayed in supermarkets will also be Halal, because anything else causes offence? What will the secularists say about *their* rights?

## 1.6 SOCIETY AT A CROSSROADS

As a society we are being ruthlessly conditioned to accept what feels like continual change (which of course was also one of the goals of the Frankfurt School, because it leads to instability). But one result of recasting these changing values as 'human rights' is inevitable competition between the different interest groups. In reality we are at a cultural and social crossroads, and Christians are being faced with a choice. We either roll over and accept the new order, in the process surrendering some of the core tenets of our faith and giving voice only to politically correct platitudes that will ensure we don't cause offence. Or we decide that our values and the Christian heritage that has informed and made our nation are worth defending, so that we make a stand. We reclaim the ground.

So what does this mean in practice, and how can we do it while at the same time maintaining the love and respect for others to which we have been called by Christ?

## 1.7 DEFENDING CHRISTIAN 'RIGHTS'

### *Rediscovering our faith*

Although it is tempting to start demanding that others acknowledge their debt to Christianity and stop attacking our rights, where this actually has to start is with ourselves – in particular, with the revival of our faith, and recommitment. Only then, when we know what we believe and why, can we begin to look outwards.

The basic problem is that we have been subjected to so much psychological conditioning over the past 50 years that many Christians – even those in ministry and leaders of the Church – simply don't know what to believe any more. However, in crumbling before secularist reframing and accepting the lie that tolerance means accepting without judgment any and all behaviours known to man – because this is what 'love' actually means – the Church in Western society has betrayed its calling. Worse, we have stood back and allowed truth to be rewritten, meekly accepting the charge of oppression and unfeeling cruelty; of exploitation of the weak for our own ends; and of loading individuals with unacceptable burdens of guilt, which God, if He exists at all, never intended. The blunt truth is that we have lost our way – to such an extent that we don't even know the truth any more, let alone how to apply it. At base we have no idea why Christ should have died, beyond some woolly notion that he was a good man, talked a lot about love, and gave us an example of how to live.

So we have to start by recovering the truths of our faith, which means that we need to return to the Bible, and then, both collectively and individually, we need to repent where we have deviated and gone astray. Because only then will we have the clarity to understand our spiritual heritage, and what God has done for us uniquely in Christ. And only then will we be able to stand against the snake wiles that twist and deny the truth.

### Standing on Truth

Second, we must stop being 'people-servers' and make a stand. We must fear God rather than man, because otherwise we consign humanity to the very destruction and death from which Christ rescued us. *This is our ground zero*. If we don't stand up for our faith, then not only do we betray the One who died for us, but we condemn our fellow human beings to unimaginable torment that will last forever. Therefore, in love, we have to stop running scared, and start fearlessly standing on the beliefs that have been handed down to us, and for which we now stand guardian.

Third, we need to claim back the language – because whoever controls language (as the 'pro-choicers' know) controls the outcome. So we must reframe what has been reframed, reclaiming what has been taken from us and restoring truth. And 'truth' is the key here. We need to start facing and spelling out the consequences of social and governmental policies – both for individuals, and for society as a whole.

For example, sex education policy since the 1960s means that we now not just accept, but even encourage, children as young as eleven (sometimes even younger) to have sex. We are told this is normal and call it one of their fundamental rights. But there are several points to be made here:

(a) Sexual activity amongst young children is not 'natural'. In the 1950s the average age for first sexual intercourse was 21,[27] while in the 1960s sexual activity amongst school children was virtually non-existent.[28] The truth is, if kids are allowed just to be kids, they won't even start thinking about sex until their mid to late teens, because they'll be too busy testing the boundaries of who they are and what it means to be human through education and play, hopefully having a lot of fun. The last thing they need is to be launched into behaviours for which they are not ready, and which will adversely bind them for the rest of their lives.

(b) The encouragement of early onset sexual activity, divorced from relationship and commitment, means that sex is no longer viewed as something special, but is rather regarded as a leisure activity, with oral or penetrative sex becoming the new goodnight kiss. This makes it very hard for girls to say no, and violence against women of all ages is reportedly increasing. But, since time began, sex has been rightly seen as one of the primary bonds cementing a man and woman together, so that the loss of meaning inherent in current attitudes causes irreparable damage to the formation of stable and long-lasting relationships. This means that families are intrinsically less stable.

(c) As a result of promiscuity, sexual infections among teenagers are now at epidemic levels, some of which can't be cured and are even life threatening. A child acquiring one of these infections, therefore, may well have it for life, and it may damage their capacity to reproduce.

(d) As a result of family breakdown, a by-product of trivialised attitudes towards sex and weakened relationships, mental health problems amongst young people are at an unprecedented high, with research now suggesting that in any given year 20% of children under the age of 16 will have a diagnosable mental health problem, mainly relating to conduct and emotional disorders.[29]

All the evidence clearly shows current policies are not working – indeed, that children are increasingly being put at risk. Standing on evidence, therefore, we need to recover the language so that we can once again reframe the debate.

### *Standing on the letter of the law*

Fourth, we need to be more vocal in claiming our rights. The Equality Act 2010[30] lists certain "protected characteristics", including age, disability, gender reassignment, marriage and civil partnership, race, religion or belief, sex, and sexual orientation. An unreasonable amount of prominence appears to be given to just a few of these characteristics, namely: gender reassignment, marriage and civil partnership, sex and sexual orientation. But Christianity, as a religion or belief, is equally included within these protections, so we need to protest when our rights are infringed, or we are discriminated against.

To put it another way, the current social bias *against* Christianity, seen in the ever-increasing number of court cases alleging bigotry and discrimination, is simply not good enough. It is a blatant infringement of democracy, of free speech, and of the *right* freely to practise our religion as enshrined in Magna Carta. We need therefore to assert our rights and, just as the opposition do, claim 'hate speech', intimidation, and discrimination against any and all attempts to silence or marginalise us. Perhaps too we should bring actions against those businesses that refuse services to Christians or heterosexuals. Such businesses most certainly exist, and it feels a violation of justice that they be allowed to continue, while the Bull guest houses and Asher Bakeries of this world are penalised and shut down!

### *'History is written by the victors.' Why history matters*

Fifth, we must stand against the rewriting of history (which means of course that we first need to know it). So often these days, things done in the past in the name of Christ are presented as oppressive acts of self-glorification and exploitation, and therefore evil. The Crusades, for example, are now routinely described in terms of Christian aggression and unjustified cruelty, but this entirely ignores the three centuries of violent Islamic expansionism and intense cruelty against Christians that preceded Pope Urban's call to free the Holy Land.

Certainly bad things were done – and where that happened there clearly needs to be repentance – but the primary impulse, which should be acknowledged, was liberation and protection, and was both justified and good. Similarly, Christians are condemned for their involvement in the slave trade – but without intense and costly campaigning in the 19th century on the part of Wilberforce (a Christian), it would never have ended! Indeed, in those parts of the world that reject Christianity, it still flourishes, with an estimated 30 million people living in slavery today.

If we allow the rewriting of history, we relinquish our heritage and Christianity will be obliterated.


## 1.8 TIME TO MOBILISE

Whatever we may tell ourselves in the interests of maintaining a quiet life, in the current ideological struggle there is no such thing as a safe middle ground where we can remain neutral. We are either on one side or the other. It is as stark as that. We either defend our rights and our faith – which, as seen in Magna Carta, has made Western society what it is – or we lose those rights altogether, and see a different, intolerant and harsh value system prevail. A system that will only allow the expression of views that validate itself, with everything else rigorously suppressed!

As Christians we are called to love. We are not called, in the name of tolerance, to accept without question or comment what we know to be wrong, on the spurious grounds that Jesus 'loved' and accepted sinners. On the contrary, we have a duty to stand both for our *rights*, and for what is right.

Those rights include the right to respect and honour, because all alike are made in the image of God. And they include the rights to life and to freedom of choice, because this is what God has ordained. Any opposing idea of rights, separated from this understanding, is necessarily both artificial and transient. It is also wrong.

Alfred the Great knew exactly what he was doing when he prefixed the Ten Commandments to his legal code, because it is our primary relationship with God that alone gives equal value and honour to the individual, and allows justice to prevail, protecting men and women against the arbitrary exercise of power by tyrants. It was an understanding shared by the architects of Magna Carta. It is for these reasons that we once again need to defend our rights.

*Endnotes*

[1] http://www.ohchr.org/EN/Issues/Pages/WhatareHumanRights. aspx

[2] http://www.un.org/rights/50/carta.htm

[3] emphasis added.

[4] *The Triumph of Christianity*, Rodney Stark (HarperOne 2011) pp. 12-14

[5] Acts 25:12

[6] Genesis 1:26

[7] Luke 12:48

[8] http://www.secularism.org.uk/about.html

[9] http://www.secularism.org.uk/religion-and-state.html

[10] http://www.secularism.org.uk/religion-in-schools.html, http:// www.secularism.org.uk/health.html

[11] "A secular approach to education would see 'faith schools' phased out and ensure that publicly funded schools are equally welcoming to all children, regardless of their religious and philosophical backgrounds."

http://www.secularism.org.uk/religion-in-schools.html

[12] "We think the teaching of creationist views as a potentially valid alternative theory to evolution is unacceptable in state schools."
http://www.secularism.org.uk/creationism-in-schools.html

[13] https://www.marxists.org/subject/frankfurt-school/

[14] See *The Frankfurt School: Conspiracy to corrupt*, Timothy Matthews 2009 http://tapnewswire.com/2012/06/the-11-recommendations-of-the-frankfurt-school/

[15] Donn Teal, *Gay Militants: How Gay Liberation Began in America, 1969–1971* (New York: St. Martin's Press, 1971), 37.

[16] New York Daily News, July 6, 1969.

[17] New York: Penguin, 1989

[18] http://isreview.org/issue/63/stonewall-birth-gay-power

[19] As seen for example in Qur'an:9:5 – "Fight and kill the disbelievers wherever you find them, take them captive, harass them, lie in wait and ambush them using every stratagem of war."

[20] 8th century collection of oral traditions of the words of Mohammed by the Arab historian Ibn Ishaq, who wrote influential biography of the prophet Muhammad.

[21] Reported in The Huffington Post, 25 June 2014. http://www.huffingtonpost.co.uk/2014/06/25/islamic-banking-bonds-sharia-uk_n_5521566.html

[22] http://www.civitas.org.uk/pdf/ShariaLawOrOneLawForAll.pdf

[23] http://www.dailymail.co.uk/news/article-2587215/Sharia-Law-enshrined-British-legal-lawyers-guidelines-drawing-documents-according-Islamic-rules.html, 23 March 2014

[24] *Daily Telegraph*, 24 November 2014.

[25] See: Judge BANS Muslim Patrol vigilantes from promoting SHARIA LAW in Britain. http://www.express.co.uk/news/uk/459782/Muslim-Patrol-handed-Asbos-banning-Sharia-Law-promotion-or-meeting-Anjem-Choudary *The Express* 14 February, 2014.

[26] http://www.telegraph.co.uk/news/religion/11402870 Grandfathers-body-could-be-exhumed-after-relatives-of-Muslim-buried-alongside-complain-he-was-an-unbeliever.html

[27] Kaye Wellings et al. *Sexual Behaviour In Britain* (1994).

[28] '(In 1963) By the age of 16, 14% of boys and 5% of girls were sexually experienced. By the age of 18, 34% of boys and 17%

of girls were sexually experienced. *Sexual Behaviour of Young People* (Schofield, 1965). Contrast this with the advice of Brook Advisory Service, a leading UK sexual health charity, endorsed by the Department of Health, that sex at 13 is now officially seen as a normal part of growing up, reported in *The Telegraph*, 27 November 2014.

[29] *Lifetime Impacts: Childhood and Adolescent Mental Health, Understanding The Lifetime Impacts*, Mental Health Foundation, 2005.

[30] http://www.legislation.gov.uk/ukpga/2010/15/contents

Chapter Two

# THE CASE FOR CHRISTIAN FREEDOMS: AN HISTORICAL PERSPECTIVE

Philip Quenby

## 2.1 INTRODUCTION

The United Kingdom in the early years of the twenty-first century remains in many ways one of the richest and freest places on earth. This nation, and those which look to it to provide models for their laws and institutions, have had a proven track record of delivering better government and greater personal freedom than has been the case over much of history and in the larger part of the globe.[1] This does not mean that all has been perfect, neither that we have never made mistakes, nor that our progress has been a smooth and uninterrupted one from darkness towards the light. Yet, taken in the round and viewed across the sweep of centuries, we are bound to acknowledge that something unique and of great value has been birthed here and then exported across the world. The issue we need to consider is why this should have happened. Were there special conditions that applied in this land which made it so, or was the development of freedom, democracy and rule of law (and the panoply of civil liberties that have grown from them) merely a matter of chance? Could these things just as well have come into being elsewhere or not at all?

The answers that we give to those questions are of

fundamental importance not only in terms of understanding the past. They go to the heart of what we are as a nation and the path that we wish to tread in years to come. Moreover, they have implications for how we engage with other cultures and belief systems both at home and abroad. The conclusions may be uncomfortable for some, since they involve turning on its head much of the current consensus about such matters. It is fashionable in some quarters to talk about culture, values and institutions as though they are somehow distinct from the ideology that animates a society. Attaining British-style freedoms is thus characterised as a development issue, the assumption being that these are things which any nation will move towards inexorably as it reaches a given level of wealth and economic progress. We have imagined that it is possible to transplant institutions and a way of life, and thereby replicate the benefits that come with them, into societies which do not share (and, in some cases, are downright hostile to) the ideas and beliefs that made these things possible in the first place. If nothing else, the failed experiments of this kind that litter the recent past should provide an incentive to delve deeper into issues that we have too often preferred to gloss over.

This is a vital task, for our nation stands at a crossroads. Ahead is a continuation of the road we have travelled for over a thousand years, a way based on Judaeo-Christian values and beliefs. To either side lead quite different paths: one, signposted, "secular humanism", denies the existence of God; the other affirms that God exists but asserts that His character and requirements are not those of the deity described in the Bible. In recent years we have turned aside from the values and beliefs that have guided us in former times, but have largely done so without an informed debate about what those values and beliefs are, where they come from, what their consequences have been and what our future direction as a nation should be. It should be evident that we can put off a proper debate about which road to follow not a moment longer. It is therefore of huge importance that we look at our history and learn from it – not so as to wallow in an imagined Golden Age that has never really existed, but because no-one can hope to find their way unless they know their starting-point, and nobody can know that unless they know where they have come from. When we reflect on what our values and beliefs are and what has brought our freedoms into being, we are also necessarily reflecting on history, because the experience of the past colours the culture of the present and the values that derive from past experience and present culture combine to set our future direction. History, culture and values – past, present and future – are all interlinked.

History and tradition can provoke mixed reactions, and it is true that old attitudes and old ways of doing things can be outmoded, old-fashioned and out-of-date. There is another side to it, though: a living link to the wisdom of the past and the accretion of national knowledge and experience. We inhabit a land so awash with history that we can sometimes be blasé about this, or fail to see what outsiders more readily recognise. There always seems to be a commemoration of some sort going on and it might sometimes appear that we have a surfeit, but that does not mean that the past is of no value or that it should be treated as something that merely affords entertainment, having no relevance for the present. It is difficult for us to gain perspective on everyday events, for we do not have the advantage of seeing how things turn out in the end. That is why the lessons of history can be so valuable: they provide a chance to see purpose where those involved saw only confusion, to see eventual outcomes rather than immediate responses and to see patterns and trends that are too often lost in the messiness of everyday activity. We need to cast aside prejudice to look four-square at the past if we are to see our way ahead clearly.

The 800th anniversary of Magna Carta in 2015 has been the cause of much celebration and a fair degree of self-congratulation, but it is of greatest importance that we do not imagine that the battle for freedom has been won once and for all or lose sight of underlying fundamentals. We must look carefully to foundations, because the foundations of this nation are under threat. What does history show to be the foundations of freedom, democracy and rule of law, three things which this nation has gifted to the world and which are commonly said to lie at the very heart of our values?

## 2.2 FREEDOM

Magna Carta is widely regarded as a foundational text of the British Constitution and an essential guarantor of basic freedoms. The first things that need to be said about it are that at the time of its birth its claim to be unique was much less obvious than passing centuries have made it seem, and that its survival was very far from being assured. The thirteenth century was an age of charters: in 1222 (just 7 years after the Great Charter was sealed by King John) the so-called Golden Bull of King Andrew of Hungary was issued, containing provisions which on their face did not look or sound so much different from their English equivalent. From 1220-31 the Holy Roman Emperor Maximillian granted charters which similarly had much in common with Magna Carta and in 1287 King Alfonso III of Aragon did likewise.[2] Yet within a relatively short time these Hungarian, Imperial and Aragonese charters fell by the wayside and are now little more than a footnote of history. By contrast, Magna Carta, originally a failed attempt to broker peace between a king and his barons, has developed into something far beyond its initial remit and has taken on a force and resonance infinitely greater than anything which those who made the monarch put his name to it ever envisaged. How did this come to be?

The answer is: happenstance, and something more than happenstance. The Great Charter was saved from obscurity by the death of King John less than a year after its sealing and the accession of his 9-year-old son as Henry III. With the country in the grip of civil war and a French army in occupation of London, William the Marshal (one of two regents ruling in the name of the boy-king) reissued the Charter which King John had abrogated almost immediately it had been sealed. Thereafter, the Great Charter was frequently confirmed or re-issued – by some counts on as many as 40 separate occasions, the last during the reign of Henry VI in 1423. These twin circumstances helped make Magna Carta what it eventually became, for the habit of re-issue made it almost an earnest of good intent on the part of each new king and ensured that it grew into a living, breathing instrument which on each re-issue came to encompass and consolidate the steady growth of freedoms which were built on its original wording. In the process, over the passing centuries the Great Charter was able to take account of and reflect developments in society at large. It is notable, for example, that the charter granted by King John in June 1215 nowhere mentions three things that in the public consciousness are now closely associated with this document: Parliament, democracy and juries. Yet by speaking of "liberties", "customs", "rights", "justice", "the law of the land" and "the common counsel of the land", Magna Carta came to embrace precisely these things.

So much for happenstance; but there was something else about Magna Carta which *was* unique and which helped provide the motivating power for extension and development of the rights and freedoms which King John's original charter first proclaimed. For the Great Charter was not suddenly summoned into being out of nowhere. It drew on and tapped into a Saxon heritage which was grounded in Christianity. The very idea of having King John seal a charter was largely the brainchild of Archbishop of Canterbury Stephen Langton, who based the charter sealed at Runnymede on 15 June 1215 on the so-called Coronation Charter which had been issued by Henry I over a century beforehand. That Coronation Charter had promised to abide by the laws of King Edward (meaning Edward the Confessor, the last Saxon king whom Normans recognised as having been a legitimate ruler). In their turn, these laws of Edward the Confessor incorporated earlier Saxon codes, including those of King Alfred the Great, and so Magna Carta preserves a direct link to Saxon England. Promising to abide by the laws of King Edward effectively meant taking over Saxon laws (and just as important, the Saxon approach to law) lock, stock and barrel. It was a repeat of the promises that William the Conqueror had made in an attempt to legitimise his claim to the English throne and gain Saxon support for his rule.

This was of profound importance for two reasons in particular. Firstly, Saxon legal codes made it clear that kings were subject to the law (a fact of which Church leaders did not hesitate to remind them when necessary).[3] By placing the ruler under the same constraints as everyone else, Saxon law carried within itself the promise of rights for the common man and thus not only the seed of what Magna Carta eventually grew to become, but also the germ of democracy itself. Rights for the common man because, if a king was subject to the law, the corollary was that a subject could rely on that same law to protect him in his dealings with the State, so the subject had rights which the State could not override. And the germ of democracy because, as time passed, it became increasingly difficult to deny political rights to subjects who had legal rights, equality in one arguing strongly for equality in the other. Secondly, the laws of King Alfred began by reciting the Ten Commandments and various other Old Testament laws. By putting God's law first and man's law second, they recognised that law is not simply what we choose to make it, but is answerable to a higher moral standard based on and derived from the Bible, and in fact the idea that a ruler is subject to the law is set out clearly in Scripture. This was the rule from the foundation of ancient Israel, as shown by the arrangements Moses put in place after the Israelites' escape from Egypt (see for example Exodus 18:24-26 and Deuteronomy 17:10-12), and it applied equally throughout that nation's later history.[4]

Limits on state power and a corresponding freedom for individuals from arbitrary or excessive use of that power were thus part of English heritage almost from the start, deriving from a mixture of Saxon customs and biblical teaching. That is not to say that the liberties now associated with Magna Carta sprang fully formed into the light: far from it – many were initially present only in the most shadowy form and needed to be developed through a process that was often painful and almost always contentious. The meaning and relevance of the Great Charter were fought over in the English Civil Wars of the 1640s, for example, when the supporters of Parliament specifically relied on it to justify their armed rebellion, but elements of it remained in issue for centuries afterwards. The very existence of a right to free speech was uncertain as late as the reign of Charles II, whose Licensing Act of 1662 prohibited the publishing of *any* work without government approval, whilst freedom of conscience was to prove a thorny problem for generations afterwards. The point, however, is that (whatever might be said on the other side of the equation) in England there was always a strong impetus towards freedom – strong enough almost to be called a moral imperative – by virtue of the way that the influence of the Bible was rooted not only in Magna Carta but in the law and in ideas of kingship.[5]

From the moment it was granted, Magna Carta held out the promise of freedom – freedom from arbitrary rule, freedom from oppression, freedom from tyranny. That was the clear implication of clause 39, which spoke of no free man being imprisoned except by the judgment of his peers or due process of law. Those provisions in their turn opened the door to other freedoms such as freedom of conscience; for what greater tyranny could there be than trying to dictate what men and women should think, of seeking to rule the inner life as well as the outer? As soon as the Great Charter set about curtailing arbitrary or disproportionate exercise of royal power, the logic of a society which was not only formed by Christian values but had these embedded at the very heart of its laws, and as a central determinant of the relationship between citizen and state, made a compelling case for the charter's original liberties to be extended and then extended again. Arguments in favour of freedom of conscience, for example, drew heavily on the fact that choice was of the essence of Christianity – the freedom to accept Christ or reject him – so that it simply made no sense to try and compel what had to be freely given; and this outlook in turn reinforced the tendency towards freedom, since choice is the enemy of dictatorship. Likewise, Christian belief in free will reinforced ideas of freedom of the individual.[6] So whilst the Great Charter is justly regarded as a guarantor of certain basic freedoms, it is essential to recognise the Christian underpinnings which helped give it birth and drive its development. These are the ultimate foundations on which the inheritance that we think of as being built on Magna Carta rests.[7]

## 2.3 DEMOCRACY

In similar fashion, Christian doctrine was massively significant in spurring the development of democracy. It was not the only influence, for Magna Carta's talk of the "common counsel of the realm" (itself building on Saxon traditions of representation in the king's council, the Witan) was also a factor, but again it was biblical teaching which provided an overarching intellectual framework and a moral imperative for the progressive extension of democratic rights. To illustrate that proposition, we can do worse than look at the so-called Army Debates which took place at Putney in the autumn of 1647 in the immediate aftermath of the first English Civil War. With Parliament victorious and King Charles I its prisoner, the Parliamentary high command sought to quell unrest within the New Model Army by inviting two delegates from each regiment to a debate before Cromwell and Ireton about what form the future governance of the nation should take. It was in effect a constitutional conference and no army in history had seen anything like it before. During the course of over two weeks, they argued for things that have since become accepted parts of the national political landscape: for regular Parliaments; for fairer electoral districts; for a man's right to vote no longer having to depend on owning a minimum value of property (property in this context meaning real estate); and for democracy based on one man, one vote – their reasoning for the latter being that the Bible said that man was made in the image of God (Genesis 1:27) and showed that in the beginning there had been no distinctions of wealth or class, so it followed that all were of equal worth and each deserved an equal say.[8]

Democracy was inseparable from the beliefs of the soldiers who came to Putney for other reasons, too: because they were passionate about giving everyone access to the

Bible and allowing each man and woman to decide for him or herself what it meant; because their model of church governance was congregational, with each individual group of believers forming a self-governing entity outside central control, thereby empowering individuals and allowing them to take part in decision-making; and because they put obedience to God before the demands of secular authorities, lessening the hold which dictatorial regimes could exercise. All of these things were at heart democratic ideals and processes, and it was beliefs of this kind which built on the seed of democracy lying half-hidden in the fact that the Great Charter made the king subject to the same law as the people. Moreover, Christianity gave intellectual cohesion to arguments in favour of democracy because that form of government presupposes the innate dignity of all human beings (a dignity which Christians acknowledge by virtue of all being made in the image of God) and also requires their ability to choose between right and wrong. It therefore necessitates recognition that there is such a thing as right and wrong, for if those concepts are mere phantoms, the decisions taken as part of the democratic process can have no rational basis.

The demands put forward at the Army Debates were not a flash in the pan. They were virtually identical to ones made almost a century later by the radical John Wilkes (1725-97), when presenting the very first Bill for reform of Parliament, and a century after that by the Chartists.[9] They are indeed a recurring theme, the voice in British history that will never quite go away. From time to time this voice has been marginalised, ignored or suppressed, but it has always re-surfaced. It is the voice of freedom and democracy – and the driving force behind it comes from the Bible. It is all too readily forgotten that when Abraham Lincoln spoke of government of the people, by the people, for the people, he was quoting directly from the preface to the first English translation of the Bible by John Wycliffe. Consequently, it is fair to say that (for all the influence that classical Greece may have had) democracy as it has developed in the West does not come primarily from the example of ancient Athens but from biblical teaching filtered through Saxon concepts of law and government. Without the logical and moral imperatives provided by Christianity, the need for and even the desirability of democracy would have been far from evident.[10]


## 2.4 THE RULE OF LAW

As with freedom and democracy, Christianity has played a pivotal role in the development of English law. The law code of Alfred the Great (incorporated into later Saxon codes and preserved through Magna Carta to play a part in the later growth of the English legal system) made it clear that English law looked first and foremost to the Bible for its inspiration. Saxon laws self-consciously attempted to align English law with biblical teaching in a way that was distinctive. One of the most far-reaching effects of this was that the relationship between ruler and subject was drawn in a very different fashion from that which applied in systems derived from the traditions of Roman law, where the same limits on executive power did not apply. Saxon law acknowledged what continental legal systems did not: that a ruler is under judgment just as much as a commoner, hence his authority is always subject to the law and his power is limited. It followed that power was not for the king to wield as he pleased, but was to be exercised for the common good. The preamble to Magna Carta made precisely this point by having King John declare that the charter had been given (amongst other things) "for the improvement of our kingdom".

Another consequence of the Saxon approach to law was the recognition that law was not something that kings could make (or unmake) at will, but was constrained by moral considerations that came from outside the law, were beyond the ability of men to manipulate and formed parameters within which law had to operate. This outlook was carried over into the English common law which started to develop in a recognisably modern form under the circuit judges of Henry I, and the common law's resulting insistence that a law should be measured not just against the formal processes that had led to its adoption, but also by reference to its moral content, is another element that made English law fundamentally different from Continental legal systems. It was precisely this heritage which enabled renowned 18th century judge and legal theorist William Blackstone to write that "Any law that is contrary to the scripture is no law at all and not to be obeyed." In making that statement, he was not expressing a wish but recording a fact – a fact which has been an essential part of ensuring that English judges have so often championed the individual against an over-mighty state instead of serving as agents of repression.[11]

Magna Carta had some vital things to say about law. It made the king promise that justice would not be sold to the highest bidder, that due process and the laws of the land would be observed, and that the right to trial by jury was entrenched. These provisions underpinned the development of a genuine rule of law in succeeding centuries, especially after the Glorious Revolution of 1688 created a truly independent judiciary by doing away with the Crown's former right to hire and fire judges at will. To the cheerleaders of the Glorious Revolution, their revolt was a re-run of baronial rebellion against King John and the 1689 Bill of Rights issued under William and Mary was a new Magna Carta. As with so many other aspects of freedom, these elements proved to be interlinked and also to be the means by which further advances towards freedom were made. For juries did not only help protect subjects against an over-mighty state. They also implicitly recognised that the people's consent was needed if law were to command not just obedience, but respect. So what Magna Carta said about law had an impact on politics, too, by bolstering arguments that a sovereign's right to rule derived from a contract with his subjects – a theory which ultimately required democracy if consent were to be seen to rest on sufficiently broad and firm foundations.

To see the radical results that this Christian-inspired concept of law was capable of producing, we need look no further than the career of one of its foremost exponents, Lord Chief Justice William Murray, Lord Mansfield. In 1772 he delivered a landmark judgment in Somersett's case, concerning the status of a black slave who had been brought to England, pronouncing: "Every man who comes to England is entitled to the protection of English law, whatever oppression he may heretofore have suffered, and whatever may be the colour of his skin, whether it is black or whether it is white."[12] The effect was that any slave who set foot on English soil was immediately free. This judgment flew in the face of all accepted convention. It came 35 years before William Wilberforce and his fellow campaigners began to stir the conscience of the nation about slavery and by some reckonings led to as many as 15,000 being released from human bondage. The moral imperative that was at work behind the scenes was made clear when this same judge said: "The eternal principles of natural religion are part of the common law; and the essential principles of revealed religion are part of the common law" or, more directly still, "English law is Christian law."

It is not generally appreciated that right up to the

modern era almost every aspect of English law came about specifically in response to Christian teaching: remove this and its foundation is gone. Sadly, this legacy and this philosophical coherence is increasingly under threat, since within the last five years English judges have for the first time begun to say that today Christianity no longer has a place in English law. In doing so, they have turned their backs on over a thousand years of history. To continue down that track would be to take away the law's moral and intellectual underpinnings, leaving it at the mercy of expediency and the utilitarian. We scarcely need the example of Nazi Germany to know where that might lead.

## 2.5 CONSEQUENCES

Freedom, democracy and rule of law are good things in and of themselves, yet they are only part of a web of rights and obligations that go to make up the full panoply of liberties undergirding modern life. In marking the progression from Magna Carta to the present day, it is hard not to be struck by how the granting of freedom in one area tended to reinforce freedom in another or lead to entirely new freedoms seeing the light of day. A case in point is provided by the early history of Methodism. When John Wesley (1703-91) first began to preach, freedom of conscience was still a very young and tender plant, and Methodists suffered ostracism, disapproval, verbal abuse and physical violence, with Wesley at times in danger of his life. Yet even so there was a noticeable change from previous ages, for there was no serious, sustained official attempt to suppress Methodism. Three and a half centuries earlier the Lollards (followers of John Wycliffe, first translator of the Bible into English) had been ruthlessly stamped out. Reformers like Latimer and Ridley had been burnt at the stake in the 1500s, Roman

Catholics hounded under later regimes and Nonconformists persecuted after Charles II was restored to the throne. The treatment of Methodism showed just how much the political atmosphere had changed.

As a result of that change, religious revival under the leadership of Wesley and George Whitefield was allowed to play out with extraordinary consequences for freedom at home and abroad. Wesley was a mentor to two of the leading lights of the campaign to abolish slavery, former slave trader turned preacher John Newton and MP William Wilberforce, and Methodists were leading figures in many of the most pressing social and political issues of the day, transforming national life. When lay preacher George Loveless organised a group of fellow Methodist farm workers in Tolpuddle to fight for better pay and conditions in 1834, they may not have thought in terms of Magna Carta's liberties and privileges, but those were in issue, all the same. When Methodists began to operate outside the hierarchy of the Church of England, they may not have aimed at social revolution, but that is what they brought about, for no longer could the aristocracy keep a stranglehold on village life, with the elder son in charge of the estate and the younger in charge of the church, for now there was another outlet for people's spiritual yearnings. When Methodists helped power the national movement for extension of voting rights that was Chartism, they may not always have known how great a debt it owed to the Great Charter and its legacy, but that debt was there, nevertheless.

The inter-connectedness of life should never cease to strike us. It is now almost impossible to disentangle the threads that led to Britain becoming a world economic and political power. Without constitutional monarchy, judicial independence would have been stillborn. Without rule of law, there would have been no secure property rights and thus less impetus for the innovation which drove first the Agricultural and then the Industrial Revolution, providing economic and financial muscle far beyond that of all rivals. Without freedom of association, there would have been no Lloyds of London insurance market (whose first members met in coffee houses) and hence less trade, which in turn would have meant less wealth and less capital to finance industrial expansion. Without political stability and due regard for creditors, higher interest would have been charged on government debt, making it harder to finance the wars whose successful outcome helped secure British dominion in Canada, India, South Africa and elsewhere. Without a free press, abuse of executive power would have lacked an important check and the free flow of information needed to underpin trust in business would have been absent. That would have biased enterprises towards tight family-held groups and made less likely the economies of scale achievable by larger firms. Without representative government, there would have been no safety valve for political grievances.

A virtuous circle has been at work for large parts of this nation's history, which should give us hope but also sound a warning. Steadily eating away at freedoms could just as easily produce the opposite effect. An assault on traditional rights and liberties has to a degree been under way for some years, but far more worrying and ultimately more deadly is the undermining of the foundation on which our entire edifice of freedom stands, namely our Judaeo-Christian heritage. This has been the target of sustained attack over a prolonged period, with the result that Christianity has been increasingly marginalised and a Christian voice is more and more absent from public debate. The history touched on briefly in this chapter shows how we all stand to lose if this process continues, for the freedoms we enjoy were brought into being by Christian teaching and are unlikely long to survive its passing.[13]

## 2.6 CONCLUSION

We need to be much more honest about where we have come from and where we are going. Pluck a flower and the bloom will soon fade. We have plucked freedom, democracy, rule of law, civil society and countless other good things from the soil of faith that nourished them. For years, we have lived on the legacy of the past, but this inheritance is fast being spent. There is all too little appreciation at present of the underlying basis for our system of government and our laws, and by extension of our freedoms and the values on which they rest. It is not merely that these were planted in an age when Christian belief was taken for granted: they are deeply rooted in Christian teaching and practice. It simply is not the case that any society might have conceived them and that only chance brought them about in a particular place and time. Collectively we may choose to deviate from the path of our forefathers, but let us make that choice from a basis of knowledge rather than ignorance, let us make it only after a proper national debate and let us not pretend that the other paths which lie before us would have delivered anything like the society we have at present. They would not and they cannot.

*Endnotes*

[1] This is no idle boast: murder statistics, which are the best proxy we have for comparative levels of violence and disorder across societies and across ages, bear it out. They show that murder rates in England were significantly below those of France, Germany, Italy, Scandinavia and the Low Countries from the thirteenth century right up to the second half of the twentieth century.

[2] The core of the Holy Roman Empire comprised modern Germany and Austria, though at various times Bohemia and Moravia (the Czech Republic), parts of Italy, the Low Countries

and even western France fell (at least nominally) within its borders. Aragon, at its height comprising the Balearic Islands, Sardinia, Sicily and a large part of the north-west of the Iberian Peninsula, was united with Castile by the marriage of Ferdinand and Isabella in 1469 to create the union of crowns which in due course became the Kingdom of Spain.

[3] In 747 St Boniface reminded King Aethelbert of Mercia that it was "not [by] your own merit but [by] the abundant goodness of God [that you were] appointed king and rule over many" whilst Alcuin told King Aethelred to "have the love of God in your hearts, and [to] show that love by keeping his commandments". The subtext was clear: kings were obliged to keep the law, just as kings in ancient Israel had been bound to do: see for example Deuteronomy 17:18-20.

[4] A king of ancient Israel was subject to the duties and limitations set out in Deuteronomy 17:14-20 and was required to "read in [the book of the law] all the days of his life ... that he turn not aside from the commandment." (See Deuteronomy 17:20).

[5] It was no accident that the English Civil War broke out when a king of Scots descent sat on the throne. Charles I was son of James Stuart, who had become ruler of England as well as Scotland in 1603 on the death of Elizabeth I. Magna Carta did not apply in Scotland and neither James nor his son saw reason to be bound by it south of the border. Like his father, Charles I espoused the doctrine of Divine Right of Kings – the idea that a monarch was appointed to rule by God and was answerable to him alone. This was directly contrary to Magna Carta and was the antithesis of English traditions of kingship.

[6] By way of comparison, the Koran states that "There is no compulsion in religion." (Surah 2:256). However, Muslims do not regard this as allowing someone to change their religion from Islam. In fact, Surah 4:89 says that apostasy is punishable by death. Muslims therefore cannot choose which religion (if any) they wish to follow. What we regard as one of the most fundamental freedoms is thereby denied.

[7] Though Magna Carta began life as a document for the elite, its rights and liberties soon began to be something on which the common people could rely, too. To make sure that its provisions were put into effect, the Great Charter had a security clause. And

this required the barons to extend to their own vassals the rights which the king granted them. Equality before the law and rights for all followed inexorably behind. Add to that the Charter's glance over its shoulder to the laws of Saxon England and to the Bible, and its potential to grow far beyond its original remit is clear.

[8] The same reasoning explains why it was ultimately impossible to resist expanding the franchise not just to all adult males but also to women. The Christian worldview sees human equality as based not only on fundamental considerations of how we are made, but also of how we are redeemed. As St Paul put it, "For it is by grace you have been saved, through faith – and this is not from yourselves, it is the gift of God – not by works, so that no one can boast" (Ephesians 2:8-9, NIV).

[9] The name derives from the so-called People's Charter of 1838, which (amongst other things) repeated earlier demands for regular Parliaments, extension of the franchise and abolition of property qualifications for the right to vote.

[10] The teaching of Islam provides an instructive parallel. Since *shariah* is regarded as complete and perfect, it is necessarily fixed for all time. In a true Islamic system a parliament would therefore have no legislative role to play as new laws will not be required and interpretation of existing laws is the province of theologians. The representative role of Parliament is similarly redundant. As with the relationship between man and God, so with relationships between men: Allah cannot be questioned or held to account, and he treats the opinions of men as being of no consequence. Since a Caliph is Allah's earthly representative, he should behave and be treated likewise. It follows that in a genuinely Muslim society there is no place for democracy in the western sense so that, at best, a parliament can be little more than a cipher.

[11] One of the reasons that the German legal establishment proved largely supine in the face of Nazi lawmaking was that they espoused the philosophy of logical positivism. This treated a law as valid if proper formalities had been observed in making it, regardless of what its moral content might be.

[12] In dramatic fashion, Mansfield was stating the fundamental English legal principle of equality before the law. By contrast, the Koran: (a) states that the evidence of two women is needed to

equal that of one man (Surah 2:282), entrenching a view of women as fundamentally inferior; (b) curses Jews ("Be you monkeys, despised and rejected": Surah 7:166) and calls them "monkeys and swine" (Surah 5:60); (c) prescribes that the *dhimmi* (Jews and Christians living under Muslim rule) should pay a tribute tax called *jizya* (Surah 9:29); and (d) enables husbands to divorce wives with greater ease than vice versa (Surah 2:228-232). In matters of sex, race and religious affiliation, therefore, equality before the law is a concept alien to Islam.

[13] There are few better illustrations of the inability of the secular humanist tradition to safeguard freedom than the French Declaration of the Rights of Man and of the Citizen of 1789. Despite its high-sounding ideals, this delivered bloodshed and military dictatorship. That it did so was no accident, such a result being foreseen by Edmund Burke and clinically exposed in his *Reflections on the Revolution in France*. The weaknesses inherent in the constitutional arrangements of revolutionary France and the strengths of the Anglo-Saxon approach were also analysed by Alexis de Tocqueville. The approach of Islam towards freedom, democracy and rule of law has already been noted.

# Chapter Three

## MAGNA CARTA: BACKGROUND AND FOREGROUND

## Bishop Michael Nazir-Ali

### 3.1 INTRODUCTION

In this chapter I survey the historical hinterland for the Magna Carta (because it didn't arise out of nowhere) and also its foreground. I then explore some issues that arise for us today as a result of the situation in which we find ourselves.

### 3.2 THE BACKGROUND

So looking at the hinterland first, what is the background to Magna Carta? Where did it come from? One of the things that is worth noting is the way in which newly Christianised kings and kingdoms in this country (because there were several of them at first) made covenants with their subjects. They gathered them together, clergy and people, and made covenants principally about two things: freedom and order, or perhaps I should say order and then freedom as the kings were very concerned about order in their kingdoms. Freedom had two aspects to it. Freedom *from* certain things – for instance from unjust taxation, arbitrary arrest, or from confiscation of land, particularly expropriation of common land. There was freedom *from* these things for the subject and then also freedom *for* certain things. There was a concern (and the bishops, if they were good bishops, were at the forefront of promoting this) that the king should promote peace in his kingdom and between the different kingdoms. As well as safety from vandalism and attacks by people who would come and destroy property and take life, there was also a concern for the administration of justice within the kingdom – freedom for that and for fairness. Those were the emphases in those early covenants that the kings made with their subjects which I think are relevant for our subject today.

Following these early covenants, we have the work of Alfred the Great. An appreciation of his work is essential if we are going to understand the importance of Magna Carta, both in its own time and later on. Alfred was principally concerned for three things. The first was to pacify the land. We tend to forget that, apart from the Danish invasions of which he was several times a victim, there was also considerable warfare between the English kingdoms that had the effect of sapping the strength of peoples in this country. Alfred's objective was to *pacify* both what was within his kingdom; his decision, for instance, not to take revenge on the Vikings so that there wasn't continual blood feuding going on was significant here. He also sought to *unify* the kingdoms, laying the foundations for the first unified English kingdom. His objectives were to *pacify*, to *unify* and then, most importantly, to *Christianise*. Alfred's common law was structured around the Ten Commandments, and we are aware how unfamiliar people have become with them! Nowadays we hear the Lord's Summary of the law, but Alfred was not only very willing to hear the Ten Commandments but to structure his own law around them, and crucially together with what he called Christ's Mercy. So where there was severity in the Law of Moses, this was softened deliberately in Alfred's Law by an appeal to Christ, for love and mercy for those who had offended. Justice is important, but justice and compassion belong together in the Christian scheme of things. That is one of the differences between the old covenant of the Old Testament and the new covenant in Jesus' death and resurrection.

After the conquest by William the Conqueror there was a return to a kind of royal barbarism. William's son, known as the Red King, did not respect any kind of law at all, confiscating people's property, taxing unjustly, enforcing a 'law of the forest' where the king pretended that he owned every forest in the land and that anyone who even shot a deer for dinner was liable for a capital penalty. Something had to be done and so when the Red King was killed St Anselm, the Archbishop of Canterbury, refused to crown the Red King's successor, Henry I, until he had sworn an oath on a charter of liberties. This Charter of Liberties is in fact the immediate background to Magna Carta. Anselm was responsible for the first abolition of slavery in this country in the Council of Westminster where anyone trading in people was threatened with excommunication. So it wasn't just Wilberforce and his allies who recognised that slavery was wrong.


## 3.3  THE CHURCH AND MAGNA CARTA

Thus we come to Magna Carta and the pivotal role of Stephen Langton. Langton taught at the University of Paris for a long time before he became Archbishop of Canterbury. His particular focus was in exploring when it is right to obey the ruler and when it is right to resist the ruler. Langton was also a Bible commentator (that is why he divided the Bible into chapters and verses). Langton did not know how relevant his studies would become, but sometimes we don't do we? It's only later on we discover that what we've done as a student or in our research suddenly becomes a public issue. It was like that with Langton, and he relied very much on the work of another scholar, John of Salisbury. Yet when he became

Archbishop of Canterbury and realised the extent of John's wrong doing, he already knew the Bible's teachings on obedience to the ruler and that in certain circumstances there is a duty to obey God rather than men. When Langton met with the barons, his fellow bishops, and indeed merchants as well, he had rediscovered Henry I's Charter of Liberties. When he showed the barons and the merchants this charter, they were astonished. Scholars know that Stephen himself drafted an early document that lies behind Magna Carta. The drafting of Magna Carta itself was more complex, but in this Langton was able to use the Charter of Liberties. Magna Carta had a chequered history and John did everything possible to try and destroy it. Langton held Rochester Castle for one year against the king. During this time Langton himself was suspended from his functions as Archbishop of Canterbury by the Pope who had switched sides to John. Summoned to Rome, he had to leave Rochester Castle in the hands of some of the barons. It is possible that if Langton had not held Rochester Castle at that time, John would have been able to renege on Magna Carta and that would have been the end of the story.

So Magna Carta did not come from nowhere. Many of its provisions had been in the Charter of Liberties and its background in Alfred's Common Law, and before that in the covenants of the English Kings with their people.


## 3.4  THE FOREGROUND

Turning to the foreground, one of the things that I hear again and again is that nearly all the provisions of Magna Carta in law have been repealed except for four, one of them being the liberties of the English Church. However, in fact many of the provisions of Magna Carta remain in force, at least as far as their spirit is concerned. For instance, the question about no taxation without the consent of the people, Habeas Corpus, trial by jury, the principle that no one should be fined in such a way as to prevent them earning their livelihood, all of these things remain. In any case, the question for us is not so much the legal impact of Magna Carta but its moral impact. The moral and spiritual impact it had on the nation, on people's thinking about important principles of liberty, justice, and fairness. Whatever else we may say about legality, the moral and spiritual impact of Magna Carta remains very much in place.

The foreground of course has to do not just with general influence. It had a particular influence on the Reformation as the Reformers were determined that people should be free to read God's word for themselves. We take that freedom for granted. Recently I was in Rome and there was a large book shop selling Bibles, with a quotation from Pope Francis saying "People should not just keep their Bibles on their shelves or in their pockets, but read them every day." If the Roman Catholic Church had been saying that in the sixteenth century history would have been very different. As we know, Tyndale stood out, along with many others, in his determination that people should have access to God's word and be free to read it for themselves. Out of that comes not only the English language, as we know it, but a fresh appreciation of the liberties of the Christian person. Tyndale and his book on the obedience of a Christian man were significant. It's a somewhat misleading title because what he was saying was yes to obedience to the authorities as far as they were not asking us to do something that God had forbidden, or were not forbidding what God had commanded.

The Bill of Rights of 1689, following the departure of James II and the arrival of William and Mary, is again a landmark and it owes everything to Magna Carta, though couched in the context and the circumstances of its own day, but widely imitated. This always says something about the importance of a document if it is emulated by other people and other places. The French Declaration of the Rights of Man (though the French Revolution was highly ambivalent), the American Revolution and the first amendments to the US Constitution (which can be seen as the American Bill of Rights) were both influenced by the Bill of Rights of 1689. Not only other documents but whole movements, for instance the movement for the abolition of the slave trade and of slavery itself, were influenced by notions of liberty in these great charters. One of the questions with which Lord Mansfield as Lord Chief Justice was faced when Granville Sharp, the great abolitionist, petitioned on behalf of a freed slave who was being taken back into slavery, was whether there was law about slavery in England. Mansfield, to his discredit, resisted saying that there was no such thing as slavery in this country. He kept giving more qualified judgments about this in other cases, but of course the fact remains there was no law for slavery because there was no such thing as lawful slavery, as Anselm recognised in 1102. The fact that English people had laws about slavery in other parts of the world is a different issue. So the abolitionists were on sure ground to start with, at least in this country. What they were against, and this is why they began their campaign against the slave trade, was the trading aspect and they were clearly able to show from the Bible why trading in slavery was wrong. For instance when 1 Timothy speaks of men stealers; well, why would you steal men if not to sell them on to somebody else?

In time, what I have called the great Evangelical Enlightenment settlement that emerged in Victorian England came about because of this commitment, both to freedom and to order. The Clapham Sect was not anarchistic. Wilberforce, if you look at his voting record, was consistently voting for bills on order, even where sometimes we might think those bills were rather repressive. They were not anarchists, they did not want disorder, but at the same time they knew that the poor in this country and the slaves abroad had been made in God's image and could not be treated by the powerful in the way in which they were being treated; hence all the programmes such as the introduction of industrial legislation, of the ragged schools and the recovery of nursing as a noble profession. The Charity Commission at the end of the nineteenth century said that three quarters of charitable institutions had been established by evangelical philanthropy. Three quarters is quite astonishing and this Evangelical Enlightenment consensus remained in place until our own day. But now it has been unravelled and very rapidly so, even in the last fifteen years before our very eyes.


## 3.5  HOW MAGNA CARTA CHALLENGES US TODAY

Finally, I would like to address some questions as this unravelling takes place. The first being, what is the relationship between a Bill of Rights, like Magna Carta or the 1689 Bill of Rights, and democracy? In the context of the Arab Spring, I said at the time and it is still true: democracy is never enough because democracy on its own, Parliament on its own, could result simply in a tyranny of the majority or in parliamentary tyranny if you want to put it like that. We have had experience of parliamentary tyranny once before. This is why a bill of rights is needed to protect people – in particular minorities, those less powerful, or further away from Parliament – to protect them from what Parliament might do in the name of democracy. This was certainly true of the Middle East in the course of the so called Arab Spring. I should say that I don't know if there really was an Arab Spring; that's a matter for a different context.

I think it is true for us now that we need those fundamental protections that Magna Carta has guaranteed us; whatever people may say about polls, focus groups, democracy or the will of Parliament. This leads me to my second point which is the relationship between conscience and positive law. There has been a long tradition of recognising conscience in this country; for instance, even in times of war, people were able to claim conscientious objection to carrying arms. Although you may not be a great enthusiast for the Abortion Act of 1967, even this Act, though in a more and more limited way according to recent judgments, recognises conscience to some extent, unsatisfactory though the Act may be from our point of view. The Human Fertilisation and Embryology Act also recognises conscience. Yet suddenly now, this new so called equality legislation and the legislation about religious hatred does not recognise conscience, sometimes enough, sometimes at all. Why is that? Is there a new attitude to law? We have a legal tradition in this country going back to Blackstone which recognises the existence of a higher law; higher than simply the positive law of the land at any one time. Yet there was a challenge to Blackstone then and that was the challenge of Jeremy Bentham: "the law is the law is the law". We cannot get beyond and behind positive law; there is no appeal to a higher power or a higher law. Again and again lawyers in government at the highest levels, when discussing the equality legislation or religious hatred legislation, have spoken to me in a way that seems to represent unreconstructed Benthamism.

So if the law is the law is the law, how is bad law to be changed? We cannot do this unless we can appeal to something that is higher and greater, and that is what Magna Carta and the Bill of Rights were doing. We will never be able to get beyond this, not the tyranny of Parliament, but the tyranny of positive law. Currently the relationship between Christianity and public policy (note that I'm saying Christianity, not Christians) is under great strain. There are many distinguished Christians involved in British politics today. We should be grateful for this, although I have to say that, with honourable exceptions of course, I have seen good Christians come into politics and end up compromised.

So the question is not just of Christians getting involved in politics, which is to be encouraged. That is not the issue. The issue is what role the Christian faith is to play in the policies and the legislation of this country. The attempt to plead that secularism is somehow neutral has to be challenged. Secularism is not neutral; secularism is another world view just like Christianity is. The question before the people of this country is which world view are they going to take in the making of public policy and the passing of legislation? That is the question. There is no neutrality; we must move beyond this myth that secularism is neutrality, it is not. There is legislation coming again and again before Parliament that requires a spiritual and moral tradition to understand the issues, whether that legislation is about the early stages of a human person, what to do with people who are critically ill or people who have lost mental capacity, or about marriage and the family. There are innumerable matters which cannot be decided unless we acknowledge some moral and spiritual tradition to which appeal can be made, from which a start can be made.

I am not arguing for privileges for any particular church, for instance, the establishment of the Church of England. Magna Carta could not have achieved what it did without the involvement of the bishops, but establishment is a different issue. Whether a church is established or not the Christian tradition is absolutely vital for the moral and spiritual welfare of the people in terms of policy and legislation. Magna Carta is a standing testimony to the riches of this moral and spiritual tradition and there are many other examples in the course of our history, but we thank God that we have this tradition to which we can appeal, which we can invoke in times of difficulty and of opportunity. We should pray that the nation will wake up to the heritage which it has.

# Chapter Four

## THE CENTRALITY OF RELIGIOUS FREEDOM

## Professor Roger Trigg

### 4.1 MAGNA CARTA

Is religious freedom important? What do we mean by it? Its legal origins in England go back to Magna Carta itself. The influence of the Charter has echoed down the years since it was first adopted by King John by the Thames at Runnymede eight hundred years ago in June 1215. Its importance has been amplified as the centuries have rolled on. It encoded the rule of law, making it clear that no one, not even the King, could set it aside. Its insistence on the due process of law, evidenced in habeas corpus, and trial by jury, is familiar to many. What may come as a surprise to those who have not studied the Charter, is that the very first item in it concerns the freedom of the Church. The Charter confirms that the English Church (*ecclesia Anglicana*) 'shall be free, and have her whole rights and her liberties inviolable'. In particular, the Charter continues, the King accepts 'the freedom of elections' in it, and wills that 'the freedom of the Church be fruitfully observed by our heirs forever'. The last clause of the Charter reiterates for emphasis the King's command that 'the English Church shall be free.'

The question of the power of the monarch over the Church had been a matter of bitter dispute for the previous fifty years, and the murder of St Thomas à Becket in Canterbury Cathedral in 1170 had been a part of that. The Archbishop of Canterbury at the time of Magna Carta, Stephen Langton, had been himself at the centre of an argument between King John and the Pope over his appointment. Matters had moved on sufficiently by 1215 for Stephen Langton to become a central figure in the drawing up of Magna Carta, and it is thought that he was responsible for the inclusion of the clause about the Church. He was himself personally named, alongside twenty-five barons, as a guarantor of the Charter.

Does all this matter today, or is it a matter of far-off history of little contemporary relevance? Certainly the idea that church appointments should be made freely by the Church rather than the Sovereign sits uncomfortably with the later history of the Church of England. On the other hand, the idea that the freedom of the English Church lay in the hands of foreign potentates, as mediaeval popes undoubtedly were, was no doubt equally curious. Can we therefore dismiss this clause as of mere antique curiosity? We should reflect on the fact that only four clauses of Magna Carta remain on the statute book, and this is one of them. Like much in the Charter, it had an influence that was to grow in a surprising manner in the centuries to come. Indeed the retired Justice of the United States Supreme Court, Justice Sandra Day O'Connor,[1] stresses the way in which the American founders drew on Magna Carta as an example of 'the more general notion of a written statement of fundamental law binding upon the sovereign state'. She gives the guarantee of freedom of religion as a specific example of an important provision of the United States Constitution explicitly drawn from Magna Carta. In this, and other respects, the crucial importance of Magna Carta and the spell it still casts was well illustrated by a special exhibition on its influence in the United States, featuring the Lincoln Cathedral copy, held at the end of 2014 in the Library of Congress in Washington DC. It showed how the Charter's provisions were widened and reinterpreted so that the freedoms it engendered have been elaborated and honoured further as time went on. As John Roberts, the American Chief Justice, put it[2] in a book accompanying the exhibition: 'The Magna Carta of 1215 contains only the seeds of what we now regard as essential liberties. But those seeds have taken root'.

It must be significant that the Charter's first concern is the freedom of the Church, just as it is significant that the first reference in the United States Bill of Rights is to freedom of religion. Many Americans, with reason, see religious liberty as the first freedom not just in history but also in importance. The Charter's view of the freedom of the English Church may be a significant distance from contemporary ideas, but it constitutes the first attempt to codify a principle that must lie at the root of all freedom.


## 4.2 WHY IS RELIGIOUS FREEDOM IMPORTANT?

Why is it that religion above all else should be picked out for special protection? In more recent centuries we have come to see that not just institutions such as the English Church, but also individuals, need protection. A liberal society places enormous stress on this. Each of us cherishes personal freedom, not least in how to live our lives, and in what fundamental beliefs to adopt or reject. Yet the more autonomy is stressed, the less attention is given to institutions which can act as buffers between us and the State. They can even themselves become objects of suspicion as sources of unwelcome authority. Without them, the individual is more defenceless against the power of the State. And it becomes more likely that the State itself will become more authoritarian. It is left as the only restraint on the whims and desires of its citizens, who may be in collision with each other. A genuinely pluralist and free society needs institutions independent of the State that can provide different forms of guidance as to how lives should be lived. They can be sources of education for children. The alternative is a state which, in fact, if not in form, is the only arbiter of what is to be deemed good and right. Even if we all earnestly desire the common good, it is crucial that different visions of what that might be are allowed to flourish.

Citizens cannot be truly free if they are not able to live according to their beliefs of what is most important. A corollary is that such freedom cannot exist if we do not have access to different forms of teaching about what is good and right. When the State alone decides, even if it is in accordance with the will of the majority, freedom is at risk and so is democracy. How do the majority gain their views to help guide the State? If they are themselves merely the creatures of the State this will be impossible. True democratic freedom demands individual freedom, and that itself must be nourished through the freedom of institutions such as churches or other religious institutions to offer guidance. The insistence by Magna Carta on the freedom of the English Church was a first step to the acknowledgement that religious institutions need to have a voice that is independent of the State. They need special protection, however, precisely because they point to a separate source of authority than that of the State or the sovereign. They can appear to be dangerous rivals to that. The authority of God is explicitly acknowledged in the preamble to the Charter when King John claims that he is confirming the Charter 'in the presence of God and for the salvation of our soul'. The State itself is thus put under divine authority, as is symbolised by the cross on top of the Royal Crown, even to this day.

This suggests that the State must never see itself as the ultimate authority. It is not even in a position to grant freedoms to its citizens out of grace and favour, since it should not have control of those freedoms in the first place. A major difference, even in Western democracies, exists between those, like France, that see the State (*la republique*) as the dispenser of freedoms and rights and those, like the United States, that see humans as being in the words of the Declaration of Independence 'endowed by their Creator with certain inalienable rights'. These just have to be recognised. For a secular society like France with its policy of *'la laicite'*, there can be no official recognition of the authority of God, or of the actions of a Creator. As a Presidential Commission on the subject proclaimed:[3] '*Laicite* (translated often as 'secularism') implies the neutrality of the State'. It cannot thus acknowledge any other power beyond itself without breaching that neutrality and, it may seem, supporting one worldview over against another.

The acknowledgement of God by the State is anathema to an atheist. That itself might suggest that its refusal to acknowledge God is not as neutral as some might pretend, but is in accordance with particular worldviews. Is it still compatible with that of the theist? The idea of neutrality suggests that it ought to be. Yet the unwillingness to acknowledge any possibility of a power superior to the State leaves us at the mercy of whatever the current policy of the State might be. Ancient battles between church and State may have at times been rival exercises of power. At others, however, they posed this question of the source of ultimate authority.

The current emphasis on human rights may be in part an attempt to restrain an all-powerful state without appealing to any transcendent realm. It may be a way in which a neutral state can still acknowledge limits on its power. Yet the irony is that such rights can only be effective if they are seen as more than the creation of a collective will, which can change, or a legislative fiat that can be altered. To be guides of action they have to be seen as existing universally and objectively, rooted in what it is to be human. They have to stem from an intrinsic notion of human dignity, and that is difficult to hold without any theistic grounding. Many, including philosophers, attempt to justify human rights on the shaky grounds they are what 'we' believe, whoever 'we' are. Since many around the world self-evidently do not have such beliefs, that is not very persuasive.

As Magna Carta indicates, and as the American Bill of Rights spells out, freedom, and protection from arbitrary rule and the unbridled use of power, starts with freedom of religion. With the development of democracy, we have come to understand, as the American founders such as Thomas Jefferson and James Madison did, that individual freedom with regard to religion is as important as institutional freedom. Not only does the Church point to an authority higher than the State, as King John reluctantly acknowledged for a time, but individual citizens must be free to follow their own consciences. They must be able to live according to what they think is most important. If they cannot do that, but have to conform to norms imposed on them, there is no freedom, and that means in turn no democracy. When citizens cannot advocate, and practise, a religious view of the world, they cannot properly contribute to democratic debate. Given that religious freedom implies the right to stand against all religion, as well as to advocate a religious viewpoint, the freedom of all citizens is vastly curtailed.

It is often claimed that freedom is indivisible. It seems hard to see how political and economic freedoms can coexist alongside major limitations on religious freedom. Religion (and its denial) concerns how we must live our lives, teaching what is worth pursuing, and what should be avoided. It will typically include ideas of human nature, and of the place of humans in the wider scheme of things. Religion is concerned with what precisely that wider scheme of things might be. If we are not free to be guided by such visions, we cannot even use our own money in accordance with our priorities.

The danger is that this could happen in an increasingly secular society. We are told, even by senior judges, that 'faith' is subjective, of concern only to those who possess it. 'Faith communities' and 'people of faith' can go their own way as long as what they say and do does not impinge on other people. Religion is made a private affair, and the public square is swept clean of all traces of it. One reason why so much focus is given to the public display of symbols, such as a cross or crucifix, is that this clashes with the preferred idea of the public, so-called neutral, space, the 'naked public square'. Yet this is not an impartial view. It refuses to take religious beliefs seriously, as claims to truth about the nature of the world and the place of humans in it.[4] From a philosophical point of view, it interprets religious beliefs as the mere evincing of private attitudes that gain no purchase on the real world. As such, it is reminiscent of, and perhaps derived from, the philosophical obsession with science as the sole standard of truth, that still exists, but held particular sway, in the guise of logical positivism, in the middle of the last century. That arbitrarily ruled out by definition meaningful talk of the transcendent. It is dangerous for social policy to be founded on such a controversial philosophical picture.

Recent research in cognitive science[5] helped to demonstrate how the basic ways we think about religion are a constituent part of the cognitive architecture of the human mind. That is not an argument for the truth of religion in general, or of any particular religion. Our cognitive inclinations may incline us to think in a way conducive to religion, but they do not tell us which religion to adopt, or whether to discard all religion as childish illusion. Nevertheless a religious attitude, in some form, seems to be the default condition of human beings. It is 'natural' to be religious. Religion is present at all places and times, and must be taken account of, not dismissed as the idiosyncratic view of a peculiar minority. Very secular societies, like those in contemporary Western Europe appear to go against the grain of human nature, and it remains to be seen how firmly established they can be.

Stifling the public manifestation of religion, and restricting it to the private, and personal, sphere, is not just a matter of stopping many citizens playing their full part in democratic life. It is also to stamp on a basic human tendency. Others may argue that it is a tendency that is unhealthy, and must be controlled. They are using their own precious freedom to argue that the freedom of others must be curtailed in the very matters that are most important to them.

## 4.3 RELIGIOUS FREEDOM IN A SECULAR SOCIETY

Those who wish to keep religion private typically see religious freedom as freedom *from* religion rather than freedom *for* religion. They see some religion, at least, as a source of danger and, rather than appearing to discriminate between religions, treat them all in the same way. This move is explicit in a book written in the context of the threat from terrorism. The writer discusses what he terms[6] 'religious extremism', saying that 'the religious extremist believes in the infallibility of his or her belief system'. He goes on to suggest that such a worldview leads to a belief in absolutes, or a rejection of compromise, together with indifference to alternative opinions. He asks, as a consequence, whether[7] 'society and government should view religious speech as inherently *less worthy of protection* than secular political speech precisely because of its extraordinary ability to influence the listener'. (His italics). Looking at the undoubted threat from Islamism, the writer even suggests that even though freedom of speech is a hallowed principle of liberal democracy, there should be a distinction between secular speech and clerical speech.

This distinction, though, is framed in a way that covers any preaching by any religious leader that goes against current fashions of democracy. Starting from a real concern with those who want to destroy Western democracy, it speedily changes into a demand that all religions conform to whatever the prevailing standards may be. The arbitrary rule of a monarch may have been replaced by the will of the people, but in both cases the ability of a Church or any other religious institution to point to a higher authority is destroyed.

Lest it be thought that such views are aberrations, in 2007 the Council of Europe recommended[8] that states not allow the dissemination of religious principles, 'which if put into practice, would violate human rights'. They added that if doubts exist in this respect, 'states must require religious leaders to take an unambiguous stand in favour of the precedence of human rights'. The irony of this is that the right to freedom of religion is itself a basic human right, recognised as such by the European Convention on Human Rights. That does not prevent many secularists from opposing religion to human rights. They assume that the latter not only do not include the former but have nothing to do with it. Yet the concern for common humanity, on which all human rights have to be based, is most often rooted in religion, and in Christianity in particular. We are all, it is believed, made in the image of God, and are equally precious.

The 2007 recommendation stemmed from the strong strand of European secularism exemplified in the French tradition. Neutrality to religion can become outright hostility and suspicion. Yet even in Europe, other views of religion see the importance in the basic structure of rights of allowing its manifestation within reason. With the title of *Tackling Intolerance and Discrimination in Europe with a Special Focus on Christians*, a new report to the Parliamentary Assembly of the Council of Europe in January 2015 seemed to suggest a fresh approach. It concentrated on the problems facing European Christians, and did not merely see Christianity as part of a wider, and more threatening, category. It further argued[9] that 'the reasonable accommodation of religious beliefs and practices constitutes a pragmatic means of ensuring the effective and full enjoyment of freedom of religion.' The suggestion would be that this had to proceed on a case-by-case basis. There are still dangers here for religion, in that the need for reasonable accommodation is qualified, since it is said that the right to freedom of religion or belief can only be safeguarded[10] 'without impairing for anyone their other rights also guaranteed by the European Convention of Human Rights'. That might allow the right to freedom of religion or belief once again to be trumped by those other rights. That is hardly what 'reasonable accommodation'[11] should mean. Religious freedom is not a right to be acknowledged only when all other rights have been met. True accommodation involves compromise on both sides, by creating a balance between rights.

There are two related criticisms of the idea of reasonable accommodation, apart from the objections of those who want to refuse any preference for a religious conscience. What, it might be said, of protection for religious groups and institutions, of the very kind given by the first clause of Magna Carta? The second objection concerns the lack of a principled approach to religious freedom, given the insistence on a case-by-case approach, which is highly sensitive to particular facts. That seems guaranteed to produce messy court cases.

Many welcome the idea of reasonable accommodation precisely because it concentrates on the individual. They would say that human rights are individual rights, and collective rights only derive their value from individual interests. Certainly reasonable accommodation is a concept that can deal with the plight of individuals, even when their conscience leads them to stricter practices than that of some who share their religion. Just because every Christian does not wear a cross or refuse to work on a Sunday, a sincere Christian can still in conscience do either. Individual divergences within groups could still be respected. Yet this is compatible with respect for the practice of a religious group as such. The freedom of the church can be seen as important as freedom of conscience for its members. Pluralism cannot flourish if individuals are left in isolation to fend for themselves.

There is an objection, too, that reasonable accommodation encourages mere fudging in particular circumstances, without adopting principles of general application. Far better, it may be said, to ensure that general laws, which bear heavily on religion, should build in exceptions where necessary, on the model of Sikhs being allowed in law not to wear motorcycle helmets. That may be sometimes possible and desirable, but rights can still clash in unforeseeable ways. Relying on exceptions built into law will be a blunt instrument that may not account for particular cases. Special arrangements can sometimes meet individual needs, when passing a blanket exception would be far more problematic. Both blanket exceptions, and sensitivity to individual cases, can be driven by the same understanding that the practice of religion, and the exercise of a religious conscience, are both an integral part of any democratic way of life. Looking at individual cases does not preclude principle, because concern for the exercise of a religious conscience itself stems from basic principle. Unfortunately too many legal cases in recent years have failed to appreciate that.

Secularism is deeply embedded in the mindset of many modern thinkers. The threat they see as emanating from religion is intimately connected with a view of religion as intrinsically irrational. There is considerable disagreement within Western societies about religion, and there appears to be no recognised procedure for settling such arguments. We cannot go into a scientific laboratory and set up any experimental apparatus to test religious propositions. That seems to make a sharp distinction between religion and science, to the disadvantage of religion. It feeds into discussions about whether particular weight should be given to the fact that a belief is religious. We rapidly seem to be reaching the point where religious reasons for belief are enough to damn the belief, or at least to deny that it deserves public respect. An American professor of law, Brian Leiter, argues[12] that many religious beliefs 'do not answer ultimately... to evidence and reasons as these are understood in other domains concerned with knowledge of the world'. He says that 'religious beliefs are based on faith', and concludes from this that they 'are insulated from ordinary standards of evidence and rational justification, the ones employing both common sense and science'.

This simple contrast between faith and reason ignores centuries of philosophical discussion about the subject. Faith is always faith in something or somebody, and what that is has to be rationally specified. It may lie beyond scientific checking, but without controversial philosophical assumptions about the reach of science,[13] that cannot show that it is irrational. Disagreement, and the lack of resolution of disputes, does not indicate that such disputes are beyond the scope of reason. People are fond of contrasting basic metaphysical views about the existence of God with simple scientific problems that can be checked in a laboratory. Once, though, we reach the frontiers of science, and start talking, as string theory does in physics, about a multiplicity of dimensions or, as some cosmologists do, of the existence of an infinite number of inaccessible universes, we may not be beyond the reach of reason. We have certainly gone beyond the bounds of common sense, as much as any religion does. The scope of human reason, while itself limited, can reach beyond normal human experience. If we stick to 'ordinary' standards of evidence, we may rule out some science as much as any religion.

Leiter is also concerned with the fact that religions typically demand what he terms categorical demands on action. 'Fanatical' adherence to doctrine appears impervious to reason, and so, again, religion is made to look positively irrational, with baleful effects. Leiter can then define faith[14] as 'believing something notwithstanding the evidence and reasons that fail to support it or even contradict it'. We are all too well aware that there are fanatical extremists at large, who are apparently motivated by religion. Other similar people can be motivated by non-religious, even atheist, ideologies. It is not the religion that is irrational but the attitudes of the fanatics. That is why we call them fanatics. Yet anyone unsympathetic to a religious outlook can judge one religion by its fanatics, and then put all religions in the same category. Leiter is tempted by that conclusion, but recognises the importance of liberty of conscience in a democratic society. He is therefore willing to put religion under the heading of conscience, but resists any idea that religion should have any special protection. It undoubtedly does under the Constitution of the United States. Most human rights charters, however, follow the United Nations, refer to freedom of 'thought, conscience and religion', and coyly talk of 'religion or belief'. The danger in this is that religion loses any special protection, and may even become a special target.


## 4.4  IS RELIGIOUS FREEDOM SPECIAL?

A secular suspicion of religion as such, and its possible harmful influence, leads many to dismiss the importance of religious freedom.  Some refer to freedom of worship, but that itself significantly narrows the scope of religious liberty, and can easily be compatible with banning it altogether from the public sphere.  If you can go to a church, synagogue, mosque or whatever, the idea goes, that is all you need for freedom of worship.  Manifesting your faith in other ways must be kept to what you do in private.  Religion remains the prerogative of the individual alone, with no right to intervene in  public life.

Leiter is not alone in thinking that religion is insulated from ordinary standards of evidence and reasoning. This forms the basis for his view that religions can claim no special protection, and are more likely than other beliefs to be a danger to society. There is a seed of truth in this, but it provides an argument for religious claims and beliefs to be firmly in the public sphere.   Not all religion is good, and there is such a thing as a pathology of religion. Religious impulses can be misdirected.  If we are unable publicly to examine and criticise religious beliefs of all kinds, even the evil ones can fester, and be unconstrained, precisely because they are out of the public eye.  The best antidote to bad religion is good religion, but religiously motivated beliefs can only be challenged if they can be manifested in the public square.

Many philosophers and others, however, would still maintain that freedom of religion is a redundant idea, because they assume that freedom of thought and conscience can deliver the same result. Freedom of religion merely gestures to a particular one form of conscience, it would be said. In his last book, the American legal philosopher Ronald Dworkin[15] urged that we abandon the 'idea of a special right to religious freedom' and talk of the more general right of ethical independence. In other words, if we have moral autonomy and can follow our conscience, that includes all that is necessary for religious freedom.

Is respecting conscience enough to give religious freedom? Does the recognition of the importance of private judgements for the individuals concerned include a proper respect for religion? By assimilating religion to any conscientious belief, we have widened the range of what can be protected. Yet the more that needs protection, the less protection can be guaranteed. What is at issue is how far all conscientious objectors to any legal provisions should gain special exemptions from, or ask for modifications of, a law. The definition of religion is very tricky, but defining conscience is going to be doubly so. Not every personal judgement made can be a deliverance of conscience. Of those that are, some will be more important than others. Which will be judged worthy of special consideration, granted that not all can or will be? The danger is that widening respect for religious freedom into respect for conscience will not involve upgrading conscience, but downgrading all manifestations of religion. If everything is to be protected, nothing will be.

This is not to say that expressions of a non-religious conscience are unimportant, or unworthy of respect. It is just that conscientious attendance at all Manchester United games is not perhaps in the same category as the refusal to kill in a war. Widening the category of religion into every conceivable manifestation of conscience will weaken the claims of conscience. A non-religious conscience can often only claim the attention it deserves when a similar religious one is also taken seriously.

Religion involves facing whether there is anything beyond this life, beyond the so-called natural world. It typically deals with the most basic questions about how life should be lived. Are there objective principles and standards, perhaps stemming from a transcendent God, against which our own puny efforts have to be judged? The dismissal by many philosophers, judges and others, of religion as a mere subjective preference, denies the core of much religion. Christianity, for example, is not about the desires and preferences of Christians. Its message is that these should themselves be subject to external judgement. We all have to be measured by something beyond ourselves, something objective.

Politicians and others delight in talking glibly about 'values'. We are told that 'British values' are important. Why, though, are they important and where do they come from? If they are merely important because we are 'British', that is hardly convincing for those who do not want to become like us, even if they live here. The problem is partly that 'values' is a word that suggests that they are held by some individual or some group. They are what people value, or hold important. The inherent subjectivism, or relativism, of the idea should be apparent. They are made like personal tastes, or if they have a collective dimension, like rules of the road. They can vary from person to person, or place to place. People have different tastes. They cannot be criticised for them. I dislike bananas, but that does not mean you should. We drive on the left, others on the right. This country values freedom and democracy. Others do not. This line of thinking makes basic principles very insecurely based, and impossible to uphold with rational argument.

Values entered popular discourse through the encourage-ment of a philosophical outlook that made a sharp distinction between so-called 'facts' and 'values'. Facts can be established by science. Values are mere human reactions to the facts. Facts are claims to truth. Values are neither true nor false. This dichotomy stemmed from a science-based, empiricist philosophy, not surprisingly the same positivist outlook that could dismiss religious statements as expressions of personal attitudes of no general validity.

Values can change with shifting fashions, because they are not based on the rock of consistent principle. Referring to them debases the claims of any religion. Christian 'values' become relevant only to Christians. Yet this denies its ability to claim truth about the nature of the world and our place in it. As such, it must influence every judgement about what is good and right, and in particular what is conducive to human flourishing. Other religions can make comparable claims. Above all, Christianity makes claims about the intrinsic dignity and worth of each human being, and their responsibility before God. These are not preferences, or 'values'. They are assertions about what is true and, if they are true, they should inform and guide every political and moral judgement.

In a pluralist society, unlike that of thirteenth century England, the truth of Christianity will be contested. Voices that deny the claims of Christianity must also be heard. The practitioners of other religions must have a voice. Yet in all this, the point is that whether there is a God or not, whether there is a life beyond this or not, whether humans have an intrinsic dignity or not, or whether animals can be just as important, are all issues that must be relevant to how we conduct our public life together.

In the United Kingdom with its Christian heritage, talk of religion will inevitably involve particular reference to Christianity. As we celebrate the eight hundredth anniversary of Magna Carta, we are reminded that even in the thirteenth century, Christianity was central to the English way of life. It was no coincidence that if the arbitrary power of King John was to be curbed, the English Church was the very first body that needed protection from royal interference. Just because religion points to a higher source of authority, it is vulnerable to those in power who have their own agenda. No totalitarian society can allow religious freedom. Indeed, when Christianity itself preaches the importance of human free will, and hence of freedom generally, it is a powerful support for democracy, and for that reason alone deserves protection in a democratic society. The neutrality of the secularist provides little defence against those who put no value on the freedoms we hold dear. Arbitrary authority has to be constrained by the rule of law. That, though, does not exist in a vacuum, but has to be nurtured, and based on objective principles, such as those of Christianity, which are themselves constitutive of a wider view of the world.

## 4.5 THE LIMITS OF MANIFESTATION OF RELIGION

Magna Carta began the long process of the establishment of the rule of law, according to which no one, not even the King, could be above the law. There must be one law for everyone. Yet once it is accepted that the law is supreme, many, quite reasonably, object to special exceptions being made. If even the most powerful are to be subservient to legal obligation, why should religious people expect special treatment, just because they do not like some aspect of the law? When laws were explicitly based on Christian principles, this was not such a problem, but in more secular societies, ordinary Christians may find it progressively more difficult to obey every law with a good conscience. This problem has surfaced in recent years over issues such as Sunday working. We need not venture into the controversial area of same-sex marriage to see examples of threats to Christian principles that are of basic importance.

Participation by medical staff in matters concerning abortion has been a difficult issue, in which the courts, even recently, have had to rule over the extent of the exemptions that have been allowed. Perhaps assisted suicide, and even euthanasia, could be made legal in the foreseeable future, and be made available under the National Health Service. Would all its employees be expected then to provide such 'services'. Would there, or should there, be exceptions for staff with conscientious objections to killing their patients? There are plenty of theorists and practitioners who would say that even there the law should be obeyed. Otherwise, it will be said, its whole purpose could be undermined if enough people refuse to implement it.

That this is not idle speculation is illustrated by the fact that in February 2015 the Supreme Court of Canada ruled[16] that a prohibition on what it coyly terms 'physician-assisted dying' infringes the right to 'life, liberty and security of the person.' That right was secured by Article 7 of the Canadian Charter of Rights and Freedoms. One might observe that the interpretation of this apparent protection of human life to suggest that one has a right to assisted suicide (and even perhaps to euthanasia) illustrates the unbounded ability of judges, wherever they are, to interpret basic rights according to the fashions of the moment. However that may be, it certainly creates a problem for many doctors, if the Canadian Parliament does not use its power simply to override the ruling. As it is, the Court's declaration was suspended for twelve months to enable the Canadian Parliament to adopt an 'appropriate remedy'.[17]

The Court recognised[18] that 'a physician's decision to participate in assisted dying is a matter of conscience, and, in some cases, of religious belief'. However, they insist that 'the Charter rights of patients and physicians will need to be reconciled'. That might suggest that a balance has to be struck. What happens when not enough doctors are willing to 'assist' dying? Will some be coerced into doing so? Might there be a reluctance to make exceptions to the general law, if assisted dying becomes an authorised medical practice? At the least, it will no doubt be expected that doctors who are unwilling to participate refer patients to doctors who will. Yet some might think that morally, if not legally, they would then become accessories to murder.

The general problem of laws and exceptions has a long pedigree. In 1878 the United States Supreme Court was faced with Mormons who wished to practise polygamy because of their religious belief. This is no doubt a case where most of us would sympathise with those who thought the law should have no exceptions. The Chief Justice[19] of the day asked whether a man's religion in such a case should excuse him, so that polygamy should be tolerated. His retort was that to permit this would be 'to make the professed doctrine of religious belief superior to the law of the land'. He added in a phrase that echoed through the next century, and was to be quoted again in the Supreme Court, that this would in effect be to permit every citizen to become a 'law unto himself'. He further thundered that 'government could exist only in name under such circumstances'.

That in essence is the appeal of a consistent rule of law, so that laws cannot be modified to meet the whims of the powerful, or even the conscientious objections of the moral. It is an argument that will be used by those who have no sympathy for religious consciences, when they interfere with delivering agreed policy. When religious people ask for special exemptions in the name of religious freedom, they are depicted as demanding exceptions, in much the same way as a powerful king might imagine that he is above the law. Arguments for religious freedom are, it will be said, merely arguments for preferential treatment.

It might cynically be added that the Christians and others only appeal to religious freedom when they find themselves in a minority. Early protagonists of religious freedom were often persecuted minorities, such as seventeenth century Baptists. Too often, too, when they held power, Christian Churches have cared too little for the freedom of those who dissented from them. These are salutary points. Christians should remember that religious freedom is a precious principle stemming from our nature as human beings, and from a Christian understanding of the purposes of God. It must not be appealed to only in a self-serving way. Christians need freedom, but so do members of other religions and of none. The defence of religious freedom should involve freedom for all even, perhaps especially for those with whom we disagree.

Ronald Dworkin concludes his championship of ethical autonomy by saying that there are many occasions when religious exemptions cannot be made without undermining, or at least damaging, the relevant policy. In such cases, he believes,[20] 'the priority of non-discriminatory collective government over private religious exercise seems inevitable and right'. Yet it is one thing to uphold the rule of law, but another to uphold the authority of government over the individual conscience, particularly when the most basic views of human life are in play. The primacy of the rule of law cannot be used to cloak the imposition of an external will, whether that of the King, or the will of the people, democratically arrived at, on its victims. True democracy is not an elective dictatorship, but springs from the conscience of each individual citizen which, it is to be hoped, is directed at the common good. As such, it must cherish the individual conscience, or it will destroy itself.

There are differing views of the good, and they all may have a serious contribution to make. They may conflict, and the purpose of democracy is to enable us to live together, even though we have deep disagreements. Democracy will not flourish through the deliberate suppression of the views of any minority. The future of democracy depends on respecting difference, and, above all, allowing minorities to live according to their own priorities, as far as is possible, within a common framework.

Religion provides the bedrock for the beliefs of many. Other forms of conscience should also be respected, but once religion is thought subordinate to the will of the State, respect for conscience soon withers. Law cannot be respected, other than as a tool of power, if it has no moral force. A secular view of a neutral law, standing apart from all possible visions of the good, is a vacuous fantasy. Even the idea that law should be non-discriminatory, dispensing 'equal justice' for all, is freighted with moral assumptions about the intrinsic worth of every human person.

The second part of Article 9 of the European Convention on Human Rights places limitations on the right to manifest one's religion or belief in the context of a democratic society. They include 'the interests of public safety, the protection of public order, health or morals, and the protection of the rights and freedoms of others'. These might seem uncontroversial, as norms, but they can be interpreted in different ways. They cannot themselves provide a neutral base to which those in disagreement can appeal for a resolution acceptable to everyone. The protection of morals is a clear example. A Christian might think that the sanctity of human life provides the basis for any moral system. Others, like the Justices of the Canadian Supreme Court, might appeal instead to human autonomy, a basic right of individual choice, or the alleviation of suffering. The criteria can hardly help determine the outcome of debates about assisted suicide and euthanasia without begging the questions at issue. The appeal to rights does not solve the problem, when one right can be simply allowed to override another.

This has happened frequently when the protection of the rights and freedoms of others is brought into the picture. Other rights can simply trump the rights to manifest religious beliefs, unless that freedom is regarded itself as a major component of any democracy. The American view of religious freedom as the first freedom stems from the view that democracy cannot be established without it. The idea of limitations being placed on freedom of religion because they are 'necessary in a democratic society' sounds impressive. The risk, though, is that the limitations can appear to stem from the idea of democracy, and the idea of religious freedom becomes a threat to the democratic ideals. The shadow of eighteenth-century atheism and materialism lies across even contemporary debates. Too often reason is made to appear the prerogative of the anti-religious, rather than shared with the religious.

No democracy can flourish without individual, and collective, religious freedom. Individual citizens have to be able to make up their own minds about what is right and good. Priorities in the establishment of public safety and order are not always obvious, and need to be subjected to searching public debate. Health itself is far being from an uncontroversial notion as a criterion. Thus the criteria given as grounds for limiting religious freedom can themselves be open to controversy, and should be recognised as such. When one, temporally prevalent, view of what is good is allowed to extinguish all others, democracy has forgotten that its role is to manage disagreement, not remove its possibility. Humans are fallible, and when one view is imposed on everyone, it is assumed that the majority are right. There are then no alternative viewpoints left as possibilities, if things go badly wrong.

One group does not have an intrinsic right to impose its views on others, and coerce them. We have to recognise that a pluralist society, in which different beliefs are allowed to exist, is the inevitable result of democracy. It is also the reason for the growth of democracy in the first place, as a way in which people of different religious beliefs can live together. The growth of religious disagreement, in forms that did not exist at the time of King John, has been the great driver on both sides of the Atlantic for a wider democracy since the seventeenth century. The preservation of that democracy demands acknowledgement of views that are far from shared by everybody. Yet beliefs that can never be manifested are worthless, and any democratic society has to be prepared to countenance, and indeed nurture, such diversity. Religion cannot trump all other considerations, but it cannot itself always be trumped or ignored. Even so, there have to be negotiated limits. The fact that polygamy is practised in some religions cannot be a conclusive reason in its favour since cogent arguments, not least about the treatment of women, can be marshalled against it. Religious views must be taken seriously, but still have to be prepared to enter democratic discussion and decision-making. Some religion can be very evil, as when it enjoins human sacrifice. Religions themselves disagree. They have to be prepared to be critically scrutinised, but should not be ignored from the outset. We must engage with them in a reasonable way, even if this sometimes means going on a case-by-case basis.

In the United Kingdom, as Magna Carta continues to remind us, the Christian voice has been a constituent part of our society from its foundation. Stopping that voice being heard, or letting it be simply overruled by the political fashions of the day, will fundamentally change what this country is. We do not start from a position of neutrality to all religion, let alone to Christianity. Reasoned debate, and willingness to compromise, and to accommodate the religious conscience in an increasingly secular society, not only ensures that we remain true to our history. We will also be preserving the basic principles of our hard-won democracy.

*Endnotes*

1. Justice Sandra Day O'Oconnor, *'Magna Carta and the Rule of Law'*, *Magna Carta: Muse and Mentor*, ed Randy J Holland, Thomson Reuters and Library of Congress, Washington D.C., p.5.

2. *Foreword to Magna Carta: Muse and Mentor*, p.xi.

3. *Laicite et Republique, La Documenation Francaise*, Paris, 2004, p.30.

4. For more on religion and claims to truth see Roger Trigg, *Religious Diversity: Philosophical and Political Dimensions*, Cambridge University Press, Cambridge, 2014.

5. See Roger Trigg and Justin Barrett (eds.): *The Roots of Religion: Exploring the Cognitive Science of Religion*, Ashgate Publishing, Farnham, 2014.

6. Amos N. Guiora, *Freedom from Religion*, 2nd ed. Oxford University Press, 2013, p.36.

7. Guiora, p.36

8. Council of Europe Parliamentary Assembly: *'State, Religion, Secularity and Human Rights'*, Rec 1804 (2007) #15.

9. Council of Europe, Parliamentary Assembly, Resolution 2036 (2015) #2.

10. Res. 2036 #6.2.1

11. For more on 'reasonable accommodation' see Roger Trigg, *Equality Freedom and Religion*, Oxford University Press, 2012, p123ff and Roger Trigg, *Religious Diversity: Philosophical and Political Dimensions*, p182ff. Also see Matthew Gibson, *'The God Dilution': Religion, Discrimination and the Case for Reasonable Accommodation'*, Cambridge Law Journal, 72, 2013, pp.578-616.

12. Brian Leiter, *Why Tolerate Religion?* Princeton University Press, 2013, p.34.

13. See Roger Trigg, *Does Science Need Metaphysics?* (forthcoming), Yale University Press, 2015.
14. Leiter, p.34
15. *Religion Without God*, Harvard University Press, 2013, p.132
16. 2015 SCC 5 Carter v. Canada
17. Carter v. Canada #125
18. Carter v. Canada #132
19. Reynolds v. US, 1878, 98 US 145 166-7
20. Dworkin, p.137

Chapter Five

FREEDOM AND THE STATE

John Scriven

## 5.1 INTRODUCTION

Issues of freedom are of great importance – to us as individuals and as a society. Freedom, particularly freedom of expression, is fundamental and is felt to be so. But what is the basis of freedom? What happens when freedoms clash, and what are the limits to freedom? What are the political challenges to freedom, particularly religious freedom, in the United Kingdom? And how do issues of discrimination and human rights fit in?

In Christian thinking, freedom is an idea grounded in the purposes of God for humankind. So this chapter considers free will, its relationship with reason and truth, and the foundations of political freedom. It goes on to consider the current challenges to freedom in our current laws and their application. Here two matters frame the debate about the exercise of freedoms, particularly religious freedoms. These are first, the power of the State generally and secondly, the application of human rights and anti-discrimination legislation, and these are considered in turn.

## 5.2 FREE WILL AND REASON

We take free will for granted. We know that we can make choices and that they are real choices. The Bible is clear on this: Deuteronomy 30:19 (KJV): "I call heaven and earth to record this day against you, that I have set before you life and death, blessing and cursing: therefore choose life, that both thou and thy seed may live." Freedom from compulsion is a condition of faith and obedience to the Christian God. And freedom exists for a purpose – not to make arbitrary and meaningless choices, but to choose the right and to live better. And there needs to be a framework of truth to make sense of these choices.

In Christian belief the eternal 'logos' is the organising principle of the universe that is part of the nature of God. While it is an article of belief for Christians that Jesus is the 'word made flesh', Western thinking generally is also grounded in the assumption of a rational (and Christians would say, created) order. For free choices to be meaningful, there must be an acknowledgement that truth exists. But truth depends upon the freedom to choose. This is because, as Immanuel Kant illuminated, free will is necessary to rationality. If we cannot make choices about what is true and what is untrue, we cannot reason. We are automatons, prisoners of our past and of our future. So rationality depends upon free will, and intellectual freedom is essential in the search for truth. This includes the freedom to reason about truth, to disagree with culture and background and to debate absolute values, including those of religion. Free will is the foundation of political liberty and later in this chapter we look at some of the current legal restraints upon freedom of expression and action.


5.3 DETERMINISM, UTOPIANISM AND THE STATE
Determinism can support the belief that human beings do not exercise free will but are merely animals, or machines, and creatures of their chemistry. If this is so, they can be conditioned and regulated by others. For those with

a utopian view of human nature, individuals do not need freedom because the functionaries of the State are capable of determining the ultimate good of society and bringing it about. On this view, the State is also the ultimate authority, since there is no recognition of any law above that of the State (this is the basis of the legal positivism that Bishop Michael Nazir-Ali mentioned in section 3.5 above). So the State believes that it can change human nature and social structures and remake society and its laws according to its own values. For example, biological gender can be disregarded, the nature of marriage changed, and parenting and families reconstructed. For many people, the result is that law does not correlate to reality. For Christians, it means that humankind, not God, defines good and evil, perhaps the ultimate temptation in the Garden of Eden. The State therefore determines and enforces what it sees as "good" in all aspects of life, including beliefs. A Christian view is that this denies the imperfection of humankind and trangresses free will and the created order. The doctrine of human imperfection is profoundly Christian and specifically Protestant, but it realistically describes the human condition, upon which any rational political theory must be based.

Both determinism and utopianism support the increasing power of the State. But, if utopianism is wrong in thinking that rulers can be given power to remake society because they are all-wise, pessimism about human nature can also give rise to oppression. Thomas Hobbes, in his *Leviathan*, thought that, without the State imposing order, the life of man would be "solitary, poor, nasty brutish and short". His belief in the corruption of human nature meant investing absolute power in the State to prevent disorder. It is no surprise that he was writing at the time of the Civil War in England. Hobbes can be over-maligned. He did not contemplate the wide-ranging powers of the State we see today. And he assumed that civil society would flourish in the areas left unmolested by the State. But, unlike the Puritan theologians of the 17th century, such as Samuel Rutherford, he did not believe that civil society has any natural legitimacy. In his view, the State should have absolute authority, on the grounds that no other restraint on the lawlessness of individuals exists.

Looking around the world today, one is tempted to have some sympathy with Hobbes' pessimistic worldview. But it is wrong because it devalues the created natural order (though the human beings that inhabit it are imperfect). And it undervalues the capacity for good in human nature and the capacity for human cooperation. It also fails to reflect observation of how communities are formed and how they function. Some years later, Macaulay criticised the political theory of J.S. Mill on the grounds that, despite the thousand and more years of politics in action, Mill never alluded to any examples of how political theory actually worked in practice.


## 5.4  HUMAN IMPERFECTION AND GOVERNMENT

The response to human imperfection should not be to increase the power of the State (as Hobbes advocated), but to limit it, since rulers can abuse their powers. In the Old Testament, the people of Israel wanted a king, a *melech*, an absolute ruler. The prophet Samuel warned them that earthly kings would exploit and overtax them, and the subsequent history of Israel bears out his warnings.

Calvin saw civil government as instituted by God to deal with human sin and restrain evil: "The usefulness of rulers is that the Lord designed by this means to provide for the peace of the good and to restrain the waywardness of the wicked...."[2] But rulers "are not to rule for their own account, but for the public good." "Nor do they have unbridled power, but power that is restricted to the welfare of their subjects.

In short, they are responsible to God and to men for the exercise of their rule."[3] Not every government is approved by God, but the institution of government is part of the divine plan: "Although dictatorships and unjust authorities are not ordained governments, yet the right of government is ordained by God for the well-being of mankind."[4]

The Christian underpinning of government and the justice system in England survived for centuries. Kelly C.B. in the 19th century case of *Cowan v Milbourn*[5] was able to say that "there is abundant authority for saying that Christianity is part and parcel of the law of the land", but this was called into question in the 1917 case of *Bowman v the Secular Society*.[6] In the 2011 case of the Johns[7], Lord Justice Munby said that "the aphorism that Christianity is part of the common law of England is mere rhetoric" and he emphasised that, in our multi-cultural society, no religion should have any precedence over another. Nevertheless, as the historian Larry Siedentop[8] (formerly a Fellow of Keble College, Oxford) has explained, Christian belief has had a profound effect upon our values. Notions such as freedom and equality before the law are distinctively Christian and it is troubling that our judges would seek to give equal worth to the values of other religions that do not share them.

## 5.5 PERSONAL RESPONSIBILITY

We see that government must be limited because of the dangers of the abuse of power that arises from human imperfection. But limited government only works if there are restraints upon personal behaviour apart from those imposed by the State. In Christian thinking, self-government and restraint are personal and social duties.

Tacitus observed that the more numerous the laws, the more corrupt the State, and Edmund Burke saw that an absence of personal restraint leads to repressive measures in government. Conversely, as Alexis de Tocqueville noted about America in the 19th century, democracy cannot function without a restraining moral framework. And, as George Washington observed in his Farewell Address in 1796, religion (for him, it was the Christian religion) is a foundation of social morality: "Let us with caution indulge the supposition that morality can be maintained without religion ... Reason and experience both forbid us to expect that national morality can prevail in exclusion of religious principle."

Individual moral behaviour makes political freedom possible and allows limited government to function properly. Where self-restraint is lacking, people acquiesce in the increasing power of the State to prevent disorder, or to deal with the resulting casualties. This is not a new problem, though its manifestations today may be serious. The pursuit of solutions to problems that should not have existed in the first place is perennial. One of the characters in Margaret Kennedy's *Ladies of Lyndon* (1923) remarks: "Dolly thinks that our much vaunted civilisation is too much preoccupied with palliatives. She's very strong upon the folly of substitutes for godly living as she calls it. She thinks we concern ourselves too much with averting the consequences of our own acts, instead of eradicating folly and vice itself."[9]

## 5.6 FREEDOM OF BELIEF AND THE STATE

Augustine described the two realms that Christians inhabit, the earthly city and the heavenly city. A Christian owes duties to each of them, but they are not the same. Jesus said "Render therefore to Caesar the things that are Caesar's, and to God the things that are God's". He advised payment of the temple tax (see Luke 20:25 NKJV and Matthew 17:24-27).

But the earthly city cannot determine an individual's eternal destiny. This must be the choice of the person concerned. So there must be a place for the exercise of conscience that is protected from political control. Society is different from the State and there are private realms into which the State should not trespass. If it does so, the State is tyrannical.

The earliest statement of belief for Christians was that "Jesus is Lord". Declaring this, or declining to sacrifice to the Roman emperor as a god, could cost a believer his life, since it denied that the emperor had jurisdiction over all areas of life, including belief. The house churches in China today are persecuted, not because of their Christian doctrine or practice, but because, unlike the state-approved church, they do not agree to being regulated by the State.

## 5.7 THE POWER OF THE STATE AND MAGNA CARTA

Magna Carta limited the powers of the monarch by consent and the acknowledgment of a higher law than that of the State. In the past, limits on the power of the government were established in English law. Lord Justice Camden, in the case of *Entick v Carrington* (1765), had to decide whether the defendants had the right under a warrant from the Secretary of State to search for, and take away, papers which the State deemed to be seditious. The principle of the case, for which it has become famous, is that: "The state may do nothing but that which is expressly authorised by law, while the individual may do anything but that which is forbidden by law".

A basis of the common law is the liberty of the individual which limits the power of government. This liberty is founded upon free will and the understanding that there is a law above law, which is God's law. As Edmund Burke put it (in his speech at the trial of Warren Hastings): "We have no arbitrary power to give, because arbitrary power is a thing which neither any man may hold nor any man can give".

We may contrast this with the vast array of specific and general powers that the State has taken to itself in recent times. Take, for example, the Localism Act 2006. This says that a local authority has power to do anything that individuals may do including:

*"power to do it for a commercial purpose or otherwise, with or without charge, and power to do it for, or otherwise than for, the benefit of the authority, its area or persons resident or present in its area".*

A feature of the unacceptable power of the State is the operation of organs of government where there is inadequate separation of powers. This is the separation of the different functions in the administration of justice: the making of the laws; the prosecution of offenders; the decision as to guilt or innocence; the passing of sentence; and the execution of punishment. In the modern State, this may be combined with secrecy and the absence of natural justice (which requires each side to be heard fairly and impartially). Articles 39 and 40 of Magna Carta enshrined the right to a fair and speedy trial by jury where fundamental rights are at stake.

Applying these principles to the modern State, the State should have no right to remove children from their parents without a fair jury trial. As discussed in Chapter 8 of *Belief and the Nation*,[1] the operation of 'child protection' procedures means that children can be removed from their parents for periods of a year or more without a trial. When the trial takes place, the parents of the child often do not have effective representation and the opportunity to cross examine the 'experts' influencing the court. And there are no juries, though the consequences for the parents will be more severe than most sentences of a criminal court.

Other examples of bodies that infringe 'Magna Carta

type' rights include the Charities Commission and regulatory bodies that can formulate the rules, prosecute, decide on the sentence and enforce it. In the case of decision of the Charities Commission, there are limited rights of appeal to a tribunal in the 'General Regulatory Chamber'. But decisions of the Charities Tribunal nevertheless appear arbitrary, and there is no jury. The NCVO website records that it endorsed the refusal of permission by the Charities Commission to a Roman Catholic adoption agency to amend its objects so as not to offer adoption to same-sex couples.

As we shall see, equality and anti-discrimination legislation derived from human rights can also restrict freedom. In a secular society, it may be thought that human rights are conferred by the State or a supra-national body, and this body can therefore limit and decide upon the priority of rights. In contrast, *Entick v Carrington* said that the State has no rights to confer, but that the individual has a natural freedom to do anything not prohibited by law. Cases involving equality and anti-discrimination legislation (which can result in people going out of business) are usually civil cases held before a judge, or employment cases (where people's livelihood may be at stake). All these infringe Magna Carta, since they are conducted without a jury.

## 5.8 FREEDOM AND THE STATE IN EDUCATION

An example of the range of powers of the State is in education, where the State can introduce personal ethical standards with which parents may disagree. The freedom at stake here is the freedom of parents to oversee the education of their children. The only limit on this should be where they advocate criminal acts, such as terrorism.

An example of the power assumed by the State is the CHIPS programme (Challenging Homophobia in

Primary Schools) which has been introduced in schools in Birmingham, Essex and County Durham. Where the subject is not introduced as "sex education", parents have no right to withdraw their children from the teaching. Government policy is that same-sex relationships and parenting are equivalent to heterosexual relationships and parenting and these are promoted. The principal mention of marriage is in the context of same-sex relationships (in the book *King and King*).

The CHIPS programme promotes gender confusion, with children encouraged to dress and act as the opposite sex. The Song "My Princess Boy" includes lines such as *"Take my hand my Princess Boy, Now dance with me"* and *"Come and play my Princess Boy"*. The phrase "Princess Boy" is repeated 12 times in the song. Children have to sing this song to each other as they dance and change partners including, dancing boy with boy and girl with girl. Here the State believes it has the right to overthrow organic biological relationships and recast human nature according to its own values.

## 5.9 PROBLEMS WITH HUMAN RIGHTS

As mentioned above, a major factor affecting freedoms is the application of human rights. From a secularist standpoint, the philosophical roots of human rights appear somewhat shallow. Questions abound. Who has the authority to confer the rights? To what creatures should they be given (why not to animals)? How are conflicts between rights to be resolved? If human rights spring from human nature, what is human nature and where does it come from? If we believe in evolution by chance and the survival of the fittest, why should all human beings have inherent equal value? And if individuals do not have any inherent value, what is the basis of human rights?

Edmund Burke was critical of rights because he saw that they could undermine the organic structures of society, as in the French Revolution. His view was that: "They are not legitimate because they have been divorced from any context of law, custom or tradition. Rather they are slogans, uncertain in their meaning and potentially revolutionary in their effects." Rights, by their nature, are a reflection of human autonomy which can be a reflection of a legitimate desire for freedom. But where rights are divorced from a context of duties, personal restraint, relationships and institutions, giving primacy to rights can bring unbalanced results. That complex context needs to include consideration of 'the common good' as well as the aspirations of the individual. In many cases involving human rights, it is the absence of this context that makes them so problematic.

In practice, human rights can be useful in some circumstances. There have been many constitutions of oppressive states which have guaranteed freedoms and then disregarded them. As the barons at the signing of Magna Carta understood, a mechanism of enforcement is necessary and the international recognition of human rights and legislation is helpful. But people should not need specific human rights that are conferred (and therefore limited) by the State in order to ensure their freedom from oppression. Freedom should be theirs by right.

Conflicting rights present a problem. People have different beliefs and aspirations, yet have to coexist. Some rights are put forward to promote the interests of a particular group, and the general nature of the concepts means that they are capable of manifold interpretations. The right to family life is an example. It can also be difficult to distinguish between human rights and economic interests.

In law, human rights are generally absolute, apart from the limitations set by the State. There is usually no scope in law for a compromise between conflicting rights, so that the winner takes all in any dispute. In English law, religion or belief and sexual orientation are both "protected characteristics" under the Equality Act 2010. But, in the UK courts (as we shall see), sexual orientation takes precedence over the Christian faith. The concept of 'reasonable accommodation' for religion or belief is considered below.

One of the problems is that human rights need to be asserted and enforced in law by those who have been prejudiced by an infringement of the rights. The weak or vulnerable may be unable to do so. Human rights legislation does not recognise that a human being has any human rights until birth. The need to assert in law a right to life, rather than requiring compliance with a duty to sustain life, means that the beneficiary of the right must have the status in law to claim it. And an unborn child does not have that status.

Moreover, substantial financial resources are often required to assert rights. The Equality and Human Rights Commission can fund litigation at public expense and claim costs from the losing side. An "inequality of arms", where one side is better resourced than the other, can enable it to intimidate the other party.

There is also a problem in the separation of rights from duties. In Christian thinking, rights are a function of the obligations owed to others, including the duties owed to God to obey Him, and to love the neighbour. If duties are owed to God, the rights do not need to be enforced by the person prejudiced, who may be unborn or incapable.

Also, if rights are personal and not dependent upon duties, people can release their rights. For example, an elderly person may relinquish a right to life and consent to euthanasia because they do not want to be a burden on their relations. But duties owed to God cannot be released in that way. The person who commits suicide cannot be released from his duty to God to continue to live by the consent of those who might be adversely affected by his suicide, even if they could all be identified and were able to give their consent (and some may be yet unborn). So it is better to recast the "right to life" as a duty to God, and a duty in law, to sustain life.


## 5.10 EQUALITY AND DIVERSITY

Human rights should protect freedom of belief for all religions, but they are not all equally beneficial to the common good. To this extent, the belief that "diversity" is a good in itself is incoherent. The case as to whether the 'church' of scientology should be awarded charitable status is a case in point. Tolerance is important, enabling people to coexist peacefully in society, but for the State to encourage diversity as an end in itself seems problematic.

For the secularist, any exclusive religious belief may be perceived as a threat to cohesion and is therefore undesirable. But tolerance should not be confused with lack of belief. True tolerance recognises the differences between beliefs. It requires understanding and respect for those with whom there are disagreements, together with a willingness to engage in discussion with generosity of spirit. Christian belief sustains tolerance, because Christians believe that everyone should be treated with respect. (But to talk of respecting a belief does not make sense. You agree or disagree with a belief, or are undecided. But you respect a person.)

Giving an equal value to all beliefs in laws and society is, in any event, impossible. Where there is a conflict, courts have to make judgments and to accord some rights priority over others. Lord Justice Laws illustrated this in his judgment in the *McFarlane* case.[10] Although he said that no belief system should have priority over another, in fact he favoured a secular belief over a Christian one. Even if judges strive to be even handed in their application of statute and precedent, neutrality in the law itself is impossible. The result has been that liberal secular humanism is promoted over Christianity in our laws and legal judgments.

The issue as to what practices should be promoted in our laws and institutions has to be framed by some view of human flourishing and the common good. Secular liberalism cannot provide a plausible source of authority, and diversity is problematic in theory and in practice. Christians can promote a society and laws founded upon moral values that allow freedom of belief and a tolerance, taking into account the public good.

## 5.11 THE EQUALITY ACT 2010

We now turn to the specific application of laws that impact freedoms, particularly Christian freedoms. Whether or not you agree with the purposes of the legislation, it is clear that freedom has been limited by anti-discrimination and equality legislation.

### *Equality legislation and the Public Sector Equality Duty*

The Public Sector Equality Duty under the Equality Act requires public authorities not to discriminate against persons with "protected characteristics". These include race, religion or belief and sexual orientation. There is also a duty on any person providing employment and services not to discriminate on the basis of the protected characteristics. But there is no duty not to discriminate on any other grounds, such as political belief, or general appearance.

The Public Sector Equality Duty also applies, in effect, to individuals working for public authorities. So, if an employee declines to provide a service provided by the authority (such as registering a civil partnership in the case of Lillian Ladele) on the grounds of Christian conscience, this may be regarded as ground for dismissal. It is not relevant that the public authority could accommodate the objection by allowing another person to deliver the service instead.

### *The provision of services and the protection of "dignity"*

To date, non-discrimination rights have protected 'human dignity' – the feelings of those affected by the alleged discrimination – whether or not they have been materially disadvantaged. An example is the case of Hazelmary and Peter Bull, the Christian bed and breakfast owners. They refused a double bed to a homosexual couple. They were found liable for discrimination and this was upheld by the Supreme Court. The Bulls only gave double beds to married couples. They applied the same rule to unmarried heterosexual couples.

But, if the policy of the owners was clearly signalled on a website and there was alternative accommodation available, the only inconvenience to a homosexual couple would be another click of the mouse. What should be only a mild irritation does not justify putting Christian bed and breakfast owners out of business. The conclusion is that the law is protecting a right not to be offended by the refusal of services, not an inability to obtain the services. This is both a denial of individual freedom and against the public interest.

## 5.12  FREEDOM OF EXPRESSION AND THE LAW

### *A Christian Principle*

Free speech is an expression of the equality and dignity given to all people.  For Christians, it is necessary both because of human imperfection (we get things wrong), and (importantly) because God has given people the freedom to explore for themselves what is truth and falsehood.  It is a safeguard of political freedom, since nobody (particularly the powerful) should be immune from criticism.  Free speech is also required for the Christian faith to be explained.

The only exceptions should be where there is an offence to public decency (discussed later), incitement to commit a criminal offence, or there is harm to children.

### *The Public Order Act*

The Public Order Act 1986 has been used to prosecute or to intimidate those whose behaviour was deemed "insulting" or "threatening", until the word "insulting" was removed in 2013.  Despite the freedom of speech clauses, there have been numerous cases against street preachers.  In most cases these have been unsuccessful, but usually after the incarceration of the suspect for some hours.

There have been some victories.  The parts of the Racial and Religious Hatred Bill (now an Act), which would have outlawed unintentional behaviour which had the effect of stirring up religious hatred, were defeated (only just) and Lord Waddington's free speech amendments were passed, and survived a number of attempts to repeal them.

### *Employees*

The law is not clear about how far employers have the right to restrict freedom of expression in the workplace.  Talking about the Christian faith in the workplace can be regarded as harassment, as in the April 2015 case of Victoria Wasteney, which may be appealed. Ms Wasteney's dismissal was upheld by an employment tribunal after she had discussed her faith with a Muslim colleague and, with the permission of the colleague, had prayed for her. This would indicate that to discuss faith with a colleague who does not share it is in effect unlawful, though lawyers will say that any case of harassment will be dependent upon the facts. However, employers and other employees should not, in effect, be able to ban all discussion of religion in the workplace. It is clear that the courts regard discussion of religion as more sensitive than discussion of the Premier League, though the reasons why this should be the case are not articulated.

Outside work, employees should be freer, but a housing association employee lost his management position and had his salary cut for posting his opposition to same-sex marriage on a social networking site. He won his case in the High Court, but taking a case to court (whatever the result) can have a chilling effect on freedom of speech.

### The internet
Under the Communications Act 2003, it is an offence to send a message by means of a public electronic network which is grossly offensive. This is the case, even if those who might find the message offensive never see it, so the Act criminalises private communications. The maximum sentence is now being increased from six months to two years.

### Free speech in schools
There is also an issue of free speech in schools. A criterion for Ofsted in grading a school is the opinions of its pupils. Ofsted Inspector Joan Hewitt, who graded Durham Free School (a Christian school) as inadequate (a decision has

now been made to withdraw funding which means that it will close) commented: "Leaders are failing to prepare students for life in modern Britain. Some students hold discriminatory views of other people who have different faiths, values or beliefs from themselves". The comment did not relate to the content or the quality of the teaching but assumed that the school should be able to, and should, indoctrinate its pupils with the views which the Ofsted inspector hoped to find.

### *Limits to free speech, and pornography*

Expressions of belief should not be restricted. However, the way an idea is expressed may be so obscene that it is right to restrain it on the grounds of public decency. Satire and ridicule are a way of expressing criticism. In the case of Charlie Hebdo, whether the extreme medium (which in some cases can be obscene) is necessary to the satirical message is a matter for debate.

Pornography and violence in online media do not express an opinion or belief, but they can harm the people who access them, particularly children. The long-term neurological effects of pornography have been studied and the effects are serious. Some murders have been associated with violent pornography. Baroness Howe's Online Safety Bill, which received its second reading in the House of Lords in December 2013, is not yet law. It would require ISPs to operate pornography filters, with the ability for adults to opt in.

## 5.13 CASES ON FREEDOM, AND 'REASONABLE ACCOMMODATION'

### *Ashers Bakery*

Two cases illustrate the effect of legislation on freedom. The first relates to the provision of goods and services and concerns the Ashers bakery in Northern Ireland. The family bakery declined to bake a cake with the slogan "Support Gay Marriage" and the logo of the Queerspace gay rights group. (Gay marriage has not been introduced in Northern Ireland, though a gay marriage enacted in England would doubtless be recognised there.) The baker's owners were taken to court in a case supported by the Northern Ireland Equalities Commission and at the time of writing the outcome of the case is awaited. It was unfortunate that Karen McArthur initially accepted the order (so as not to cause a scene). She then consulted an elder in her Presbyterian church and afterwards said that they could not carry out the order. However, this should not be relevant to the outcome of a case of discrimination (though it could be the basis of a claim for breach of contract).

There are two important aspects to the case. The first is factual: the bakery was not refusing a service to gay couples and so they were not discriminating on the basis of sexual orientation. They would have baked a cake other than a wedding cake, or a cake without a slogan, for a gay couple. As David Schofield QC, representing the bakery, put it: "The defendants neither knew nor cared about Mr Lee's sexual orientation or religious beliefs, or his political opinions. The issue was the content of the cake." They were not even discriminating against Mr Lee on the ground of his political beliefs, though this is permitted under the law. (A Labour Party organisation is entitled to refuse employment to a person on the grounds that the applicant supports another party, since political belief is not a 'protected characteristic' under the Equality Act.) However, they were declining to provide a service because they did not want to support a cause. The second point is that, as illustrated by the *Bulls'* case mentioned above, the law currently protects 'dignity', or feelings of offence, and not the ability to receive a service. This applies to many, if not most, discrimination cases. The people who wanted the cake could have gone elsewhere and probably did so, but this is unlikely to be relevant to the outcome. If the Court finds against the bakery, the owners may go out of business (since they will not go against their conscience). The result would be that the law prioritises hurt feelings over the freedom to run a business.

Under the Northern Ireland Freedom of Conscience Amendment Bill it would not be unlawful to withhold goods or services "so as to as to avoid endorsing, promoting, or facilitating behaviour or beliefs which conflict" with "strongly held religious convictions". Similar legislation in the rest of the UK has been rejected by the Government.

### *Reasonable accommodation for conscience*
There is a proposal that there should be a statutory requirement of "reasonable accommodation" for issues of conscience. There is a Canadian precedent (their Human Rights Act of 1985) and there have been cases since. Baroness Hale rejected the concept when the point was put to her in the *Bulls'* case in 2013, though it can be argued that the *Eweida* case in the European Court, in effect, allowed it (Nadia Eweida's right to wear a small cross was upheld). Baroness Hale has subsequently appeared to be more sympathetic to the concept.

By analogy with the abortion exemption, there should be an absolute exemption in the case of issues relating to the beginning and end of life. However, following the *Scottish*

*Midwives* case,[11] the abortion exemption needs to be more broadly defined.

A general requirement of reasonable accommodation should work where an employer can accommodate the conscience of an employee without inconvenience and without cutting across other rights (such as in the *Eweida* case). However, where there is a requirement for public officials, teachers, other employees or foster carers to approve same sex relationships, or where the Public Sector Equality Duty under the Equality Act needs to be qualified, specific drafting may be necessary to protect conscience.

Specific drafting may also be required in the case of any refusal of goods and services to a person having the protected characteristics (such as sexual orientation). A refusal to provide goods or services on the grounds of sexual ethics would be taken to infringe the dignity of the person seeking the goods and services. The infringement of dignity, and not the ability to obtain the goods, is what the law and the courts have protected to date, since it has been irrelevant in law whether or not the services could be obtained elsewhere. Since general wording in relation to reasonable accommodation may be problematic when it reaches the courts, an exclusion (such as under the Northern Ireland Bill) would be preferable. This idea has already been rejected by the Government. If the reasonable accommodation concept is to be carried forward, the drafting should be tested against the relevant cases.

A requirement for reasonable accommodation for religious belief would (probably) not require the belief itself to be reasonable, except in extreme cases. And, in the current climate, Christians would not want the courts to rule on the reasonableness of Christian belief. But we should be aware that, under the Northern Ireland Bill (which provides an exclusion) and also with a requirement for reasonable accommodation, there may be a call for a multiplicity of beliefs to be accommodated.

### *Freedom of speech: Garron Helm*

The second case involves freedom of speech. In November 2014 one Garron Helm who, significantly, did not have the option of a jury trial, was sentenced to four weeks in prison for anti-semitic abuse against MP Luciana Berger in a Twitter post. Some people who organised a demonstration to support Mr Helm were arrested and their property searched, the allegation being that they had conspired to cause criminal damage. There was no indication that Mr Helm or his supporters were threatening violence or stopping anybody doing anything.

Helm was saying nasty things. His tweet showed a Holocaust-era yellow star superimposed upon the MP's forehead, and "#hitler was right". But his conviction offends the principle of freedom of speech. A concern is that the law could be used to criminalise other statements, for instance those that are deemed "homophobic".


## 5.14 CONCLUSION

Christian freedoms, important as they are, need to be connected with other Christian values in society. Personal self-restraint and support for the organic institutions of society, founded upon Christian values, enable a free society to operate successfully. Self-governance relieves the secular power of the need to govern behaviour by coercion.

Christian values are good for society because Christianity has a realistic, but nevertheless hopeful, view of human nature. This is: that we are made in the image of God, but we are fallen. We have free will and are capable of both grandeur and degradation. God is not constrained by the laws of nature and is a free moral agent. In the image of God, we have been given free will, and free will is a condition of moral action. But our imperfections have profound consequences for ourselves as individuals, and for government and society. All human beings are equal under God, and they are all fallible.

There is a created order in society without the State, though the institution of government is given by God. God has given guidance for individuals and societies, and obedience leads to understanding. We need the laws of God (and for Christians, His supernatural help) to guide our personal behaviour, and to help us to exercise both self-restraint and compassion.

Rulers are imperfect, as we are. Their power must be limited and power dispersed among institutions. (So there should be separation of powers.) We do not have the right, or the wisdom, to remake society in our own image. We should not coerce reality. Christians would say that the further we, as a society, stray from the God-given natural order, the worse things will go for us. Rulers should, for their own benefit, and for the protection of the people they rule, acknowledge that there is a law above law, that is, the law of the Creator.

Larry Siedentop has called the conflict between Christianity and secularism Europe's "undeclared war" – "as tragic as it is unnecessary".[12] He describes secularism as believing that: "an underlying or moral equality of humans implies that there is a sphere in which each should be free to make his or her decisions, a sphere of conscience and free action".[13] He attributes these values to Christian belief and our Christian heritage. Christian values of freedom, equality, reciprocity (treat others as you would want them to treat you), compassion, humility, self-restraint and forgiveness should be common ground with a wide section of society.

These qualities allow freedom of belief and a tolerance of different faiths where these can be accommodated, taking into account the public good.

However, other Christian principles are not widely accepted, particularly in relation to marriage, the family and abortion. But, in our plural society, Christians need the freedom to practise their faith and to persuade others to share their beliefs. For Christians, their values reflect the created order and the designs of the Creator for humankind. Because they do so, they promise freedom for individuals and wellbeing for society.

*Endnotes*

[1] John Scriven, *Belief and the Nation*, Wilberforce Publications (2012), p.191ff.

[2] Calvin, *Commentary on St. Paul's Epistle to the Romans*. The version quoted is not referenced but an accessible version is available, translated by John King, Forgotten Books (2007), p.359.

[3] Calvin, op. cit. p.360

[4] Calvin, op. cit. loc. cit.

[5] *Cowan v Milbourn* [1867] L.R. 2 Ex. 234

[6] *Bowman v the Secular Society* [1917] A.C. 406

[7] *R. (on the application of Johns) v Derby City Council* QBD [2011] EWHC (Admin)

[8] Larry Siedentop, *Inventing the Individual, The Origins of Western Liberalism*, Penguin Books (2015)

[9] Margaret Kennedy, *The Ladies of Lyndon* (1923), Virago Modern Classics (1981), p.215

[10] *McFarlane v Relate Avon Ltd* [2010] EWCA Civ B1 (29th April 2010)

[11] *Greater Glasgow and Clyde Health Board v Doogan and another* UK Supreme Court [2014] UKSC 68

[12] Larry Siedentop, op. cit. p.360

[13] Larry Siedentop, op. cit. p.361

Chapter Six

# THE APPLICATION OF SHARIA LAW IN THE UK

The Baroness Cox

## 6.1 INTRODUCTION

I seem to spend half my life in a jungle, a desert or half way up a mountain.

The nature of my work often requires me to enter war zones under fire, visiting peoples off the radar screen and largely out of sight of the world's media.

As you might imagine, the level of suffering in places like Nagorno-Karabakh, southern Sudan, Burma (Myanmar) and Nigeria is altogether overwhelming.

Yet the courage of those in the midst of persecution not only brings great hope and inspiration, but also serves as a constant reminder that we, here in the UK, are fortunate to live in a democracy which cherishes the fundamental principles of freedom and justice.

It is easy to forget, but our culture, laws and institutions all embody values which so many other nations still aspire to. We enjoy some of the most efficient provisions for transparency and accountability to be found anywhere in the world.

Such liberties are hard-fought for. They must not be taken for granted. Rather, we must be vigilant in identifying and challenging threats to these most precious freedoms.

This chapter seeks to address one such threat in our

country today. While it is not able to respond to all of the associated complex and sensitive issues involved, it does present a timely opportunity for consideration of some redress for victims suffering from serious gender discrimination, intimidation and abuse. At the very least, I hope it will generate a more widespread debate about how best to engage with the current situation in which many British citizens are being denied the rights to which they are entitled.

## 6.2 THE PROBLEM OF 'COURTS' THAT ARE NOT COURTS

Pressure on the UK court system has increased the use of alternative methods of dispute resolution, such as arbitration and mediation.

Arbitration is where two or more parties agree an independent person who will decide their dispute, with a decision which is usually final and binding, and can be enforced by the UK courts under the Arbitration Act 1996.

The Act allows parties to agree how civil disputes should be resolved, including choosing to resolve disputes according to the law of another legal system. (This allows multi-national companies to resolve disputes in the UK in accordance with the laws of other nations – a very valuable export for our country.)

This same flexibility permits arbitration to operate according to Sharia principles, therefore allowing parties to settle certain civil (often financial) disputes according to Sharia law in such a way that the decision can be enforced in UK courts.

Mediation, on the other hand, ideally involves a neutral facilitator trying to help two or more parties to a dispute to reach common ground. This mutually satisfactory agreement can sometimes be put before a court. In mediation, the third party does not decide the matter, but helps the parties to settle their dispute between themselves.

The bodies which are commonly referred to as 'Sharia Courts' appear to operate in a number of guises. Some fall within the arbitration framework, able to make legally binding decisions in legitimate arbitration proceedings.

However, there is a concern that even when these tribunals are functioning within the terms of the Arbitration Act, they are embedding discrimination against women.[1]

Of course the freedom to decide disputes in accordance with religious beliefs is something that must be vigorously protected. If a woman genuinely and voluntarily accepts a discriminatory judgement with full knowledge of alternatives available in civil law, then she has the right to do so.

But when discriminatory decisions are validated by the force of the law, particularly where women may be unaware of the implications or pressured into accepting rulings based on gender discrimination, then the law itself is brought into disrepute.

Moreover, some arbitration tribunals appear to be adjudicating on matters well outside the arbitration framework, for example, by deciding cases relating to the criminal law, such as those involving domestic violence and grievous bodily harm.

In 2013, a BBC Panorama investigation uncovered evidence of Sharia Councils in Britain putting Muslim women "at risk" by pressuring them to stay in abusive marriages. The programme showed an Islamic scholar at Leyton Islamic Sharia Council telling an undercover reporter only to report domestic abuse to the police *"as a last resort"*.[2] When the footage was shown to Nazir Afzal, Chief Crown Prosecutor for the North West and himself a Muslim, he said: "I'm disappointed but not surprised. Most of them [Sharia Councils] are fine but there are some clearly like this who are putting women at risk."[3]

British Indian author and journalist Edna Fernandes, after her own investigation, concluded that *"scores more imams dispense justice through their own mosques"* and that "*Sharia is being used informally within the Muslim community to tackle crime such as gang fights or stabbings, bypassing police and the British court system*".[4]

It has been estimated that there are "at least" 85 Sharia forums in the UK.[5] As far as it is possible to ascertain, the Sharia courts or councils appear to keep scant records, and there is no right of appeal. There is nothing like the control over justices' appointment and conduct that applies within secular courts.

## 6.3 THE PROBLEM OF INTIMIDATION

At the heart of both arbitration and mediation is the crucial matter of consent. In arbitration, both parties must agree to submit their dispute to a mutually agreed third party for a decision to be made. In mediation, the two parties are voluntarily using a third party to help them to reach an agreement that is acceptable to both sides.

However, there are widespread concerns regarding the consent given prior to Sharia Court hearings: women are often pressured by their families into going to these courts and may lack knowledge of both the English language and their rights under British law;[6] refusal to settle a dispute in a Sharia forum could lead to threats and intimidation, or being ostracised and labelled a disbeliever;[7] and going to the police or non-Muslim professional and legal sources is often considered culturally unacceptable and 'shameful'.[8] Furthermore, some Muslims may not even want to involve secular authorities.[9]

There is a particular concern that women face pressure to withhold or to withdraw allegations of domestic violence. Several women's groups say they are often reluctant to go to the authorities with women who have run away to escape violence because they cannot trust police officers within the community not to betray the girls to their abusing families.

## 6.4 THE PROBLEM OF 'MARRIAGES' THAT ARE NOT MARRIAGES

Most Sharia 'Courts', when dealing with divorce, are doing so purely in a religious sense. They cannot claim to be a civil court able to grant civil divorce; they are simply granting a religious divorce in accordance with Sharia law. In many cases this is all that is necessary for a 'divorce' anyway – although a religious wedding ceremony has taken place, the marriage has never been registered and is therefore not valid in the eyes of the civil law.

This creates a very serious problem: women who are married in Islamic ceremonies but are not officially married under English law can suffer grave disadvantages because they lack legal protection. What is more, they can be unaware that their marriage is not officially recognised by English law.

The situation was most recently highlighted in a 2014 report by the Muslim women's rights organisation 'Aurat: Supporting Women', which also unveiled cases of women in Britain living in polygamous marriages, sometimes unaware that the marriages were to a husband already involved in a polygamous marriage.[10]

The evidence for the report's findings was drawn from 50 case studies of Muslim women living in the West Midlands:

- Around 90 per cent of those who identified as being 'married' were not in marriages legally recognised by English law. Of these women, over half were not aware that they do not have the same rights as they would have with a civil marriage.

- Some of the women interviewed assumed that, because the Nikah (Islamic wedding ceremony) had taken place in the UK, it automatically counted as a valid marriage.
- Two thirds of those who identified as being married said their 'husband' has more than one 'wife'.
- In mainstream Islam, a husband does not have to undertake the same process as the wife when seeking a Talaq (Islamic divorce). He merely has to say "I divorce you" three times, whereas the wife must meet various conditions and pay a fee.
- Some of the women interviewed, when speaking of their own Talaq proceedings, specifically referred to their lack of legal protection after discovering that their Nikah did not constitute a valid marriage under English law.

As was summed up in a report by Women Living Under Muslim Laws:

*"Many women in Muslim communities in Britain believe (and men who know better can benefit by failing to correct their error) that a marriage in a mosque or before imams in Britain constitutes a valid marriage. In the event of a dispute and an attempt to enforce their rights through British courts, they are shocked to discover that, unless married in one of the very few mosques registered as places for civil ceremony, they are not validly married in the eyes of British law."[11]*

## 6.5 TESTIMONIES

I have sat with oppressed and abused women from communities which foster this kind of discrimination, here in this country, and wept with them as they told their stories.

In an attempt to demonstrate the suffering endured, I have been able to share some of their testimonies below.[12]

What is clear from the outset is that the situations described are just the tip of the iceberg. As will become apparent, the very nature of the problem means that it is difficult to provide evidence of its scale. Many women who would be able to testify about their experiences are simply too afraid to identify themselves.

One brave woman, Sami, was born and raised in the Middle East. She married very young and had four children. When her husband died, she was left with no inheritance and two of her daughters were forced into marriage at the age of 16. Meanwhile her third daughter fled a forced marriage, whilst her son escaped to Jordan at the age of 11, alone. Sami eventually sought asylum in the UK. She explained:

*"A leader of my community visited me and told me that he wanted me to marry Khaled. I felt under enormous pressure to accept his proposal.*

*The Imam told Khaled and me that he required permission from a male guardian from my family before he could marry us. I told him that I am in my late 40s, I have travelled all over the world, faced death on numerous occasions, provided for my children and supported male members of my family. 'I have grey hair – what kind of mentality is this?' I said to him. The Imam insisted that he was applying Islam.*

*Khaled travelled to Jordan to gain written permission from my 11-year-old son, who represented my guardian according to the Imam. My son's written permission stated that I could marry Khaled. I received a copy of my son's letter and I still have a copy of it. I agreed to the marriage at the Imam's home.*

*On reflection, I decided that I could not marry him due to his traditional mentality. I gained an annulment.*

*Everyone should be made to abide by the same rules. Women's rights are compromised by the operation of Sharia law in the UK. Sharia Councils often permit polygamy. Men have multiple Nikahs (Muslim marriages) and have multiple wives to gain sex and/or money. Polygamy is not about protecting women.*

*If women marry through an Imam and they eventually have a problem with their marriage, they will be forced to go back to an Imam and discuss the problem; these women feel intimidated. Many women are unable to discuss their personal issues with an Imam; they feel embarrassed and do not feel comfortable talking to a total stranger about personal issues.*

*I am in contact with large numbers of women who have a language barrier. They are not in contact with the wider community and they have no understanding of the laws available to them. Instead they believe the lies that their husbands tell them. These women, unable to speak English, are tied to unhappy marriages and have no way of accessing their rights. If a legal dispute arises they go to a Sharia Council and consult an Imam, they are not aware of the English legal system, nor are they ever informed of their rights under English laws.*

*Like me, many Muslim women are asylum seekers. They have fled their home country to live a safe life, they are running away from oppression and persecution that they suffered in their home country. They should not arrive in the UK to be met with further oppression through the operation of Sharia law. The Government should ensure that everyone in the UK abides by the English legal system.*

*For these reasons I am totally against Sharia law in the UK. The law should not be left to religious men to manipulate women in a democratic state. It is the responsibility of the Government to make sure that everyone in the UK submits to the law equally. I am worried because the Government and people outside the Muslim community are frightened to address sensitive issues like Sharia law, when the wellbeing of the majority is more important than the sensitivity of the minority."*

Sara is a British national who was forced into a marriage with Abdul, from Pakistan, in order that he might gain British citizenship. Eventually she became pregnant with his child in Pakistan and was able to return to the UK to await her husband's arrival. However, the marriage soon broke down. Sara ensured that he return to Pakistan and rapidly gained a civil divorce through the British courts.

*"In early 2000 I applied to an Islamic-Sharia Council in London to obtain a Sharia divorce. Despite all the time, money and emotional energy that I spent, and the fact that Abdul is remarried with a child, over 10 years later the Islamic-Sharia Council still refuse to give me an Islamic divorce.*

*The Sharia Council 'judges' did not listen to a word I had to say. They did not look at me when they were talking to me, rather they would look at the floor. It was awful. I felt like a second class citizen.*

*I took a copy of my civil divorce to the Sharia Council. However they were not interested in this information. They explained that they wanted Abdul to present his case.*

*The first time the Sharia Council wrote to me they pressurised me to go back to Abdul and continue the marriage despite my protests. After I refused to reconcile with Abdul, the Sharia Council wrote to me a second time and told me that I should continue living as married and not apply for a divorce. I told them this was an unsatisfactory resolution.*

*The Sharia Council eventually wrote to me for the third time and informed me that they would only grant me a divorce if I agreed to the following conditions:*

*1. To sign an affidavit, a legal document which stated*

*that I would allow Abdul to have access to my daughter. I had to agree to pay for Abdul to visit England once a year to see our daughter and to pay for my daughter to visit Pakistan once a year to have contact with Abdul. I simply could not afford this.*

2. *I must agree to a 'cooling off' period to see whether the marriage could be reconciled. I explained that I had not seen Abdul in five years and that I just wanted to obtain an Islamic divorce and to move on with my life.*

*During my civil divorce, Abdul wrote a long letter to my solicitor stating that he had no intention of providing financially for our child. This letter was used as evidence in the England and Wales courts and was thus extremely helpful in gaining a civil divorce. When I showed the same letter to the Sharia Council they informed me that the letter was not relevant to my case.*

*The registration fee cost £100. The Sharia Council would then ask me to pay £30 for every letter they wrote. The Sharia Council asked me to pay a further £200 so that my case could be heard before the panel. I refused to pay any more money. Within six months of applying for the civil divorce I gained a decree absolute. The civil route certainly upheld my rights as a woman. The civil route was so easy and more importantly, I was respected."*

Sania is also a British national. She lived in Pakistan between the ages of seven and thirteen where she was a victim of sexual abuse within the family. At the age of 16, before she had completed her GCSEs, Sania was taken to Pakistan and forced to marry her cousin, Janaid, in order for him to gain British citizenship. She was subjected to rape and physical and emotional abuse perpetrated by Janaid. Eventually she involved the police and gained the strength to leave Janaid. The UK courts made a number of orders to protect Sania and her daughters (including non-molestation orders and forced marriage protection orders).

*"I applied to the Dewsbury Sharia Council for an Islamic divorce. I was informed that the process takes a maximum of three months. It's been two years and I still haven't obtained a Sharia divorce.*

*During the continued lengthy divorce process, I spoke to the leader of the Sharia Council a number of times over the telephone. On every occasion he was unprofessional and intimidating. They questioned everything that I said to them.*

*I asked the Sharia Council to contact my UK solicitor who would hand over my legal files and copies of the court orders to the Sharia Council, which would then make them understand why I want a divorce so desperately. They viewed the UK court orders in place to protect me and my children from Janaid as irrelevant when applying for a divorce.*

*Janaid replied to my application for an Islamic divorce stating that he had been a good father. Janaid stated that he would not give me a divorce as divorce is un-Islamic and is a sin.*

*The Sharia Council then informed me that I needed to attend the Sharia Council along with Janaid. I informed them that I am not allowed to go anywhere near Janaid, I am in danger of my life, there are a number of injunctions against him prohibiting him from going anywhere near me. This is another example of their blatant disregard for UK court orders and the trauma victims' experience having been battered by their husbands. Despite my protests, the Sharia Council arranged a form of mediation for Janaid and me to attend. I did not attend. The Sharia Council refused to accept the fact that I was in fear of my life as a justification for not attending the mediation. I asked whether it would be possible for someone to come to my house. They said, no.*

*The Sharia Council then insisted that I brought along two*

*Muslim witnesses to attend the Sharia Council with me to confirm that I was telling the truth. However, Janaid did not require any witnesses because he is a man. I did not know any Muslim women who could be witnesses and I didn't want to get anyone from my community involved. In total I paid the Sharia Council in Dewsbury £170."*

In July 2000, Miri's parents decided that she was going to get married at the age of 19. This was a crucial time for Miri as she had just gained employment as an office junior in an international IT company and hoped to continue with her studies and career progression. Miri's parents took her to Pakistan where she was emotionally coerced into marrying Mohammed. She returned to England two weeks after her marriage and applied for a spousal visa for her husband, enabling him to settle with her in England. Eventually Mohammed arrived in England but he found it difficult to accept that his wife worked and wore western clothing, which led to arguments and tension within the marriage. Emotional abuse became physical abuse. When Miri's family discovered that she was a victim of domestic violence at the hands of Mohammed, she was encouraged to leave the marriage and to rebuild her life.

*"I knew I had to bite the bullet and face the fact and get it sorted. So I took the first steps of ringing around and finding out how to obtain a Sharia divorce. I was advised that it would be easy to just ring my local mosque and see if they would send a scholar or an Imam down who would chat to the both of us and get me the divorce I want. It all seemed straightforward but little did I know it was far from it.*

*When I contacted the Imam he said there was nothing he could do for me. He said there was no number I could contact or no one else he knew that could help me. I was new to this and it was extremely hard to accept and adjust to the concept that this was going to be my battle and I had to be strong for my family and my kids.*

*I found a Sharia Council telephone number on the internet. Eventually when I got through to them they said I had to complete an application form and pay a fee of around £100. Thinking that the procedure would be straightforward it was far from it. It was a battle that was to commence and continue for 2 years!! Emotionally I was drained, mentally shattered and physically tired already. Once my application was accepted I had to ring every other day just to find out the process due to their lack of response. I still didn't give up, if anything this was making me stronger and determined to fight more. I wanted justice!!*

*A month after submitting my application I received my first letter to say they had received my application and it had been forwarded to the correct department. The Sharia Council then sent out another letter that I had to fill in.*

*By this time two months had gone by and very little had been done. I received a request to send proof of my husband's whereabouts. Luckily for me, my Sharia case was running in conjunction with my civil divorce. My solicitors had all the proof but this then meant that I had to arrange another appointment with my solicitor to get this letter written up confirming my husband's address. Every time a job was done it would set me back by a month and prolong the case.*

*The Sharia Council had sent my husband three letters with no reply. This, in my eyes, should have been enough for a divorce but not for them. Even after the last letter they said they had to give him a three month cooling off period to comply or respond.*

*Then I was sent a letter to say that I had to give him full access or, if not, hand over my children for him to raise!!!! This was the ultimate blow for me as I felt I had been waiting all this time only to be told that my children will be taken away from me and my family. I thought my life had ended and I was thrown into deep water and there was no way out. I was told that if I didn't accept this then my divorce could not go ahead. I was at the same time in court for the contact for my children with my husband. The courts and the Children and Family Court Advisory and Support Service who were independently going through the case to resolve this in the best interests of the children said my husband was not to have any contact with the children. In court he accepted this without argument due to the level of violence involved. When I told this to the Sharia Council they wanted evidence, so I sent them all the court documents.*

*As far I was concerned the Sharia Council had all the required documents and there could be no reason to refuse. Then a letter came stating that I had to return the entire dowry I had in order for the final process. I then wrote back saying that I no longer had the gold jewellery stated on the Nikah (marriage certificate) because all the jewellery had already been sold by my husband in order to pay off his debt. His letter was taken into account and only then was I granted my certificate. It was a long road which I feel should not have taken so long. The pain and stress was unnecessary. I feel I was let down by the Sharia Council and demeaned just for being a woman. And what shouldn't be forgotten is that all this time not only was I suffering but also my children and my family."*

## 6.6 CONCLUSION

The problems outlined above come back to one central principle: there must be equality for all under the law of the land. At several key points, the operation of Sharia law principles in the UK today is undermining that principle.

In an attempt to highlight this unacceptable situation, and to alleviate the suffering of these women and girls, I have introduced a Private Member's Bill – the Arbitration and

Mediation Services (Equality) Bill – into the House of Lords.

Granted, its title is rather turgid, but it does seek to tackle some of the more flagrant injustices outlined in this chapter. It does so, principally, by trying to ensure that Muslim women are protected from discrimination and intimidation, that there are legal obligations on statutory authorities to try to ensure that all women know their legal rights and that any attempts by individuals or organisations to establish a parallel legal jurisdiction in this country are prosecuted as unlawful.

The Bill already has strong support from parliamentarians of all parties as well as Muslim women's groups and organisations concerned with the suffering of vulnerable women.

Yet the Government has so far refused to support it on the grounds that there is no need for its provisions, as all citizens can freely access their rights. As the testimonies above quite clearly show, this 'de jure' right is not a 'de facto' reality. Many Muslim women are unaware of their legal rights and can live in closed communities with pressure not to seek 'outside' professional help which could invoke 'shame' or 'dishonour' for their families or communities.

It is therefore crucial that we continue to discuss ways in which the rights of Muslim women, and the rule of law, can be upheld.

I hope that such conversations will promote a positive response from the Government and from key institutions such as Churches Together with a far more wide-ranging investigation to ascertain the scale of suffering endured.

I cannot sit comfortably on the privileged red benches of the House of Lords in the British Parliament whose buildings enshrine memorials to the suffragettes, when I know women in this country are suffering in ways which would cause those suffragettes to turn in their graves.

*Endnotes*

[1]   For example, a Muslim Arbitration Tribunal in Nuneaton adjudicated on an inheritance dispute between three sisters and two brothers. In accordance with Sharia law principles, the men were given double the inheritance of the women. See *Coventry Evening Telegraph*, 9 September 2008.

[2]  BBC Panorama, Secrets of Britain's Sharia Councils, 26 April 2013

[3]  BBC News Online, '*Are Sharia councils failing vulnerable women?*', 7 April 2013

[4]  *The Mail on Sunday*, 5 July 2009

[5]  MacEoin, D, *Sharia Law or 'One Law for All?*, Civitas, June 2009, p. 69

[6]  Sharia Law in Britain: A Threat to One Law for All & Equal Rights, One Law for All, June 2010, p. 16

[7]  Loc cit.

[8]  Brandon, J and Hafez, S, *Crimes of the Community: Honour-Based Violence in the UK*, Centre for Social Cohesion, 2008, pages 116 and117; Aurat: *Supporting Women, Equal and Free?: 50 Muslim Women's Experiences of Marriage in Britain Today*, December 2014, p. 12

[9]  For example, Fatwas (a Sharia legal judgement or legal opinion) have been issued which claim that Sharia law takes priority over secular law, see MacEoin, op. cit. pages 70-72; A poll of 1,000 British Muslims found that six per cent do not think that "Muslims in Britain should always obey British laws", see BBC Radio 4 Today Muslim Poll, 25 February 2015, Table 9, p. 9.

[10]  Aurat: Supporting Women, Op cit, pages 7 and 8

[11]  Warraich, S A and Balchin, C, *Recognizing the Un-Recognized: Inter-Country Cases and Muslim Marriages & Divorces in Britain,* WLUML, January 2006, p. 2

[12]  Testimonies were first recorded in the report: Proudman, C R, '*Equal and Free? Evidence in support of Baroness Cox's Arbitration and Mediation Services (Equality) Bill*', May 2012. Names of some of those giving testimony have been changed to protect their anonymity; not all time-sensitive references have been edited since the report's initial release.

Chapter Seven

# EXERCISING RELIGIOUS BELIEF AND CONSCIENCE IN TWENTY-FIRST CENTURY BRITAIN

## Robert S. Harris

### 7.1 OBJECTIVES

In this chapter I examine how cases in which restrictions placed on the manifestation of Christian beliefs and conscience are incompatible with human rights, and conflict with the tolerance, pluralism and its sister doctrine 'diversity', underpinning liberal democracy, especially when competing rights are at play. I attempt to highlight how the evidence of an apparently rife 'religious illiteracy' among the judiciary, government, public authorities and private employees is, in the cases to be studied, detrimental to the manifestation of the dual right to both hold and practise religious beliefs.

Finally, possible remedial responses are suggested to these problems which include: addressing what I call 'institutional religious illiteracy', legislating for reasonable accommodation, while also providing legal protection from workplace codes of conduct used to *override* legally enshrined religious rights.

### 7.2 PRELIMINARY CONSIDERATIONS

According to the 2014 *Religious Freedom in the World Report*, which studied the world's religions in 196 countries, Christians were found to be the "most persecuted religious minority".[1] Actual persecution in oppressive regimes is evidenced when attempts to openly practice religion can attract serious stigma, fines, imprisonment and even death. Perhaps unsurprisingly, questions of religious liberty in modern Britain sometimes attract denials that UK Christians are persecuted,[2] or the caution that some legal cases involving discrimination of British Christians is at risk of reinforcing a victim mentality.[3]

If real persecution is elsewhere, the argument sometimes deployed is that threats to UK religious liberty can be either misplaced or overstated. But being expected to act contrary to one's conscience at work, and the subsequent risk to or loss of livelihood, for those feeling in good conscience, unable to comply, are no light matters. The burgeoning body of cases surfacing has been described as the "tip of the iceberg".[4] If we were to include other fields of education and the wider societal impact of equality and diversity policies, whose reach has affected every facet of society, the volume of cases becomes very great and brings up freedom issues of the utmost gravity.

UK Christians hold freedoms of worship, assembly and conversion but it does not follow that an absence of the worst persecution renders the question of UK religious freedom redundant or of little importance. Our benchmark to gauge UK religious liberty will be human rights and the democratically inspired values of tolerance and pluralism.

Historically, and still very much true today, the realisation of religious liberty for Christians in the public and private sphere has often been squeezed between two unequivocal, biblical imperatives.

First, Christians are instructed to be law-abiding. The Apostle Paul states: "Everyone must submit himself to the governing authorities…".[5] On the question of submitting to the authority that collects and administers taxes, what Jesus said is as relevant today as it was during the first century: "Give to Caesar what is Caesar's, and to God what is God's".[6] In other words, payment of state taxes, alongside the money Christians donate voluntarily to the Church should be attended to with unstinting commitment.[7]

Second, the preeminent theme running through the Bible is that Christians are called to always put God first in all choices, commitments and actions. In response to hostility to Christians who promulgated Christian teachings, Peter and the Apostles said: "We must obey God rather than men!"[8] When asked which of the commandments are the greatest, Jesus answered unequivocally: "Love the Lord your God with all your heart and with all your soul and with all your mind…And the second is like it: 'Love your neighbour as yourself.'[9] The demands of holding dual citizenship, namely the values and obligations of the earthly and spiritual realms, have always brought challenges to Christians who seek to be law-abiding, a contrast St Augustine drew between the two domains of the heavenly and earthly city.

The positive dimension embodying the commandments defining Christian life is often obscured by what Christians are said to oppose, instead of what they unreservedly affirm. As a response to their faith, UK Christians offer 23.2 million monthly voluntary hours, in support of all types of people in the community,[10] a fact whose ramifications attract little to no newsworthiness in the secular press. In view of an often disproportionate media treatment of legal cases involving what Christians are said to be against,[11] a warped picture is conveyed, overshadowing the biblical promise of a full life.[12]

## 7.3 PUBLIC VERSUS PRIVATE

Steve Kettell, a politics scholar, believes: "Debates over the role of religion in the public sphere look certain to be one of the central and defining areas of political life in the 21st century."[13] For current purposes, "public life" or public sphere, in contrast to the "private" is assumed to include employment scenarios, in which moral and legal dilemmas relating to questions of the manifestation of faith arise for employees. To separate these as necessarily mutually exclusive is tantamount to asking practising Christians to only be true to their intrinsic identity and values inside their homes, and to repress, conceal or be ashamed[14] about their identity and its manifestation in public, a prospect at serious odds with a pluralist democracy extolling tolerance and the competing voices of diversity. The European Court of Human Rights (Strasbourg Court) has noted the 'vital' role that constitutes a believer's identity and his or her conception of life.[15] The approach to understanding the legal cases under scrutiny in this chapter involves first considering the place of pluralism and tolerance in society, followed by a look at human rights and the drive to secularise society. This is intended to provide the context for understanding the four cases studied further below. It is crucial to consider this wider cultural drama before approaching a study of individual court rulings.


## 7.4 PLURALISM

In its most simple and broadest meaning, a pluralist society is understood as one in which numerous co-existing communities freely hold to their own values, while also openly living out their identities. In the democratic context, the theory is that these groups, subject to the rule of law and the fundamental freedoms enshrined into human rights law, qualify for a platform for their voices to be heard, while also partaking equally in the wider society. The "diversity" so often celebrated and promoted in contemporary society is an offshoot of pluralist thinking. "Diversity" in the workplace has, in theory, become both an affirmation and inclusive promotion of different identities and lifestyles.

Some critics have attempted to argue that Christianity fails to qualify for a "seat at the public table on the grounds of fairness and plurality" because its asserted "right to equal participation in the public sphere" is shaped by the "unique and particularizing claims about Christianity as a major source of morality…".[16] If such a view is designed to suggest Christianity's claims are biased as a "major source of morality" and therefore lack merit, other worldviews like humanism, it should be noted, are no less biased or slanted.

There is a belief in humanist circles that the "dogma" and "fundamentalism" of Christianity renders it unsuitable for any public dimension at all. This crude and intolerant thesis conveniently ignores the very real potential in humanist philosophies for their own brand of dogma.

Critical theorist Stuart Sim, who describes himself as a post-Marxist sceptic, argues there is "fundamentalism" in numerous areas including, among other subjects, religion, politics and economics.[17] He believes "fundamentalists" whether on the right or left, are guided by their "script". What we might note here is that philosophical doctrines of moral relativism or humanism each have their own premises and reference points. In this sense, they are not free of presuppositions or a 'script'.[18] Whatever one makes of these other doctrines, we hear little of their adherents being expected to justify their theses in the way being suggested for Christians.

## 7.5 TOLERANCE

For the pluralism of modern democratic society to work, toleration is a necessary test. Humanist campaigner and philosopher A. C. Grayling wrote that tolerance is "the recognition that there is plenty of room in the world for alternatives to co-exist...."[19] We might add that, for employers, the practice of tolerance must inevitably include people with values and beliefs that may be 'disliked'. 'Liking' or 'agreement' cannot be the benchmark of when tolerance is to be shown toward specific groups. Rather, tolerance involves a litmus test of allowing space or accommodation for those with whom we may not agree.

The pivotal place of tolerance in our society is summed up by Eamonn Butler, Director of the Adam Smith Institute, who wrote: "If Britain stands for any single virtue, it must be tolerance".[20] Emma Duncan, deputy editor of *The Economist*, believes that "Britain is not just more tolerant than it was, it is also more tolerant than pretty much everywhere else."[21] Since 2014, English law officially designates religious 'tolerance' as one of the fundamental 'British values'.[22] But in terms of religious liberty, is the existence of tolerance said to broadly characterise our society borne out by the evidence? The current study testifies to a culture operating intolerantly.

Co-existence between competing lifestyles and beliefs has become an aspirational and expected part of many Western societies who profess tolerance as an 'article of faith'. But while tolerance can include 'live and let live', if it is not to be depleted of meaning, it cannot be equated with moral compliance or acceptance.

## 7.6 HUMAN RIGHTS IN CONTEXT

Our context is Article 9 of the European Convention on Human Rights, enshrined in the 1998 Human Rights Act - as it applies to holding and practising Christian belief. Article 9 (1) states:

*Everyone has the right to freedom of thought, conscience and religion; this right includes freedom to change his religion or belief and freedom, either alone or in community with others and in public or private, to manifest his religion or belief, in worship, teaching, practice and observance.*

For purposes of the four UK cases studied below, which are but a small number of the many now emerging,[23] we focus on two crucial parts of Article 9. First, there is the right to freedom of thought, conscience and religion which includes the freedom to change one's religion and belief. Second, there is the right, either individually or corporately, publicly or privately, to *manifest* religious belief in "worship, teaching, practice and observance."

The Strasbourg Court held that the rights enshrined within Article 9 constitute "one of the foundations" of a democratic society. It noted that "pluralism [is] indissociable from a democratic society, which has been dearly won over the centuries…" and depends on recognition of such rights.[24]

## 7.7  ARTICLE 9 (2): QUESTIONS OF LIMITS

It is difficult to meaningfully speak of the first part of Article 9 (1), without accounting for the second which makes it a binary right. All too often, legal disputes arise where it is thought that while people hold the legal right to a religious belief, they do not always have the equivalent right to manifest it. Artificial lines separating a belief from its application in practice can reveal both insensitivity to and lack of literacy in religious beliefs. James Eadie QC, who acted for the UK government in four Strasbourg cases, effectively argued for the separation of religious belief from its manifestation when he said: "There is a difference between the professional sphere where your religious freedoms necessarily abut onto and confront other interests and the private sphere."[25]

Importantly, Article 9 (2) provides caveats:

*Freedom to manifest one's religion or beliefs shall be subject only to such limitations as are prescribed by law and are necessary in a democratic society in the interests of public safety, for the protection of public order, health or morals, or for the protection of the rights and freedoms of others.*

Article 9 (2) acknowledges the rights of legislators or courts to restrict the manifestation of religion or beliefs, as prescribed by law, and necessary in a democracy, in the interests of a range of criteria, including the competing rights and freedoms of others.

Lord Bingham, the first person to occupy the roles of Lord Chief Justice, Master of the Rolls and Law Lord, wrote in his book, *The Rule of Law*:

*…you may believe what you like provided you keep your beliefs to yourself or share them with like-minded people, but when you put your beliefs into practice in a way that impinges on others, limits may be imposed…*[26]

Lord Bingham gave examples of when acceptable limits could apply: the self-immolation of widows on their husband's funeral pyres or female genital mutilation. Christianity would treat such practices as barbaric, yet the gist of keeping "your beliefs to yourself" still manages to cast a disturbing shadow on the basic fundamental freedoms of religion and freedom of speech.[27] How, for example, would this apply to street preachers, or employees politely offering their colleagues prayer – scenarios that have become the subject of legal disputes? By comparison, would people be expected to keep their political or other beliefs to themselves and only "share them with like-minded people"? Presumably the answer is no. Why, then, in a pluralist society, should expression of religious beliefs not hold an equal footing accorded to other beliefs?

Several of the Strasbourg Court's judges have noted

the little known fact that "conscience" is "conspicuously absent" from Article 9 (2)[28] and for good reason: the "right to conscientious objection, which is one of the most fundamental rights inherent in the human person – [is] a right which is not given by the Convention but is recognised and protected by it…". Conscience, they explain, "enjoins a person at the appropriate moment to do good and to avoid evil." The judges explained that while conscience can be "nurtured by religious beliefs" it is not always the case since people without religious beliefs or affiliations make judgments of conscience on a daily basis. It seems this is a point often missed in legal arguments involving the rights of religious claims.

## 7.8    TYRANNY OF THE PRESUMED MAJORITY

Of the 59.3% of the population of England and Wales declaring themselves "Christian" (2011 Census), there is probably no less than a large minority holding to orthodox "less popular" beliefs. There is the view that this 'minority' must not be accorded much ground in so far that 'majority' sentiment is offended. The extent to which decisive public opinion exists on any matter is often taken to suggest that public policy and law should reflect the presumed consensus. Yet this is problematic and less than straightforward in a democracy and runs the risk of oppressing, silencing or marginalising views deemed to be in the minority. It leads to an outcome, in what is now that famous phrase, of the "tyranny of the majority".

In the spirit of democracy, a diversity of voices is accommodated, not because the State or private employees are conferring their approval of certain ideas but simply by virtue of the pluralism that is said to define modern democracies.

George Orwell wrote that "If liberty means anything, it means the right to tell people what they do not want to hear."[29] The question of what is said to offend the 'majority' view is far too subjective and cannot feature as a test of 'acceptable' speech because the person or group defending the assumed 'majority' view is partial. However, defamation or an incitement to murder or violence cannot be tolerated, if the rights and freedoms of others are to be sufficiently protected.

## 7.9  SECULARISM AND THE DRIVE TO ALIENATE CHRISTIANITY

Claims that Christianity is met with militant secularism or hostility[30] are not without foundation. The Peer Matt Ridley wrote in his *Times* column[31] that belief in God is a "virus", that evangelical Christianity is one of the more "virulent infections" and that "rationalists no longer expect to get rid of religion altogether...they aim only to tame it instead, and to protect children from it". He even associated "radical Islam" with "radical Christianity." In a similarly disturbing vein, in a *Manifesto for Secularism*, signed by over forty activists, including Peter Tatchell, A. C. Grayling and Terry Sanderson, President of the National Secular Society, the "Christian right" in the US and Europe is bracketed alongside Islamist terrorist groups.[32]

Trevor Phillips, when he was head of the Equality and Human Rights Commission, said that the people "driving the revival and success" of "conventional churches" believe in "old-time religion" that is "incompatible with modern, multi-ethnic, multicultural society."[33] If "multicultural" is to mean 'pluralist', then these remarks are contradictory. Christians are as much a part of the diverse social fabric as those with secular, "modern" values.

Former Archbishop of Canterbury Dr Rowan Williams seemed to accurately sum up the government approach to religious faith under New Labour, believing it was seen as an "eccentricity…practised by oddities, foreigners and minorities."[34] The "We don't do God" stance during that period of government seemed not to have changed in any concrete way under the coalition government, beyond a shift in government rhetoric from ministers. In one notable case when a court ruled it unlawful for prayers to be said at the start of local Council meetings,[35] the government responded promptly with legal changes allowing Councils the choice to have prayers said.

## 7.10  EXERCISING BELIEF AND CONSCIENCE IN THE WORKPLACE

***Visible Displays of the Cross: the Case of Nadia Eweida***[36]
Ms Eweida worked as a member of the check-in staff for British Airways (BA). Her job required her to wear a uniform. She wanted to wear a small and discreet, plain silver cross visible over her uniform as a personal expression of her Christian faith. While BA permitted her to wear her cross, they forbade her to display it visibly. Religious items could be worn visibly if they were deemed as religiously "mandatory". Approved items included the hijab, turban, as well as the skullcap which the Employment Appeal Tribunal noted "*some* Muslims, Sikhs and Jews respectively believe they are obliged to wear." [emphasis added] Ms Eweida insisted on visibly wearing her cross after being told to conceal it, and was then sent home. BA offered her a job without public contact and the need to wear uniform, in which she could display her cross but she rejected this, regarding the cross as the central image of her faith. While

acknowledging that the visible wearing of the cross was not a faith requirement, she still considered it as a personal expression of her faith.

Ms Eweida initially brought claims of direct and indirect discrimination on grounds of religious belief, as well as harassment discrimination, which all failed. The single claim of indirect discrimination was advanced to an Employment Appeal Tribunal and then to the Court of Appeal but was dismissed by both courts.

Following a stream of adverse publicity, BA announced a review of its uniform policy. While its Chief Executive claimed BA was "proud of the diversity of its staff", he also announced the uniform policy needed to change "in the light of the public debate".[37]

In Ms Eweida's first hearing, evidence was heard from some Christians who argued against the wearing of crosses being a faith requirement, a point not disputed by anyone. One vital question generated by this case is: what is the meaning and place of the cross in Christianity? At the very heart of the Christian faith is the belief in Jesus Christ, as the Son of God, who made reconciliation between man and God possible by atoning for human sin, through crucifixion on a cross, dying and then rising to life. The apostle Paul explains that "if Christ has not been raised, your faith is futile; you are still in your sins."[38] Without this unique and one-off work of atonement, the central 'plank' upon which Christianity stands would be absent.

With this said, what is the importance of wearing crosses (or crucifixes) for Christians? There is no requirement to wear crosses, but Neil Addison, National Director of the Thomas More Legal Centre and a barrister specialising in discrimination law, has observed:

*The Second Council of Nicaea in 787 noted that: "the sacred and life-giving cross is everywhere set up as a symbol," and for millennia the wearing of a cross has been regarded as a traditional practice of Christians even though it has not been formally required as an obligation of faith. As such it is entitled to the same legal protection as the Muslim hijab or Sikh turban.*[39]

The big issue in this case hung on the legal question of whether a finding of indirect (religious) discrimination could be supported by evidence of one solitary case or whether at least two cases were needed.[40] Lord Justice Sedley in the Court of Appeal argued that to suggest there were others like Ms Eweida was hypothetical, which raises the question: was the uniform code capable of dissuading Christians from wearing visible crosses? He acknowledged there could be people who sought to avoid a confrontation and were thus deterred. In all likelihood this view seems probable.

Of about 30,000 BA employees, Lord Justice Sedley agreed with the Tribunal that since no one at BA had requested or demanded to wear a cross, it could thus not be inferred there were other Christians who were also suffering the same disadvantage. Ms Eweida's counsel had argued that on a balance of probabilities, there were others like her, and that it was an error in law to look for evidence of "group disadvantage", namely, where it could be found that Christians as a "group" suffered an actual disadvantage at BA, a position rejected by the Court of Appeal. But Lord Justice Sedley noted how, by contrast, solitary cases of disability discrimination were protected by the 1995 Disability Discrimination Act.

He was not sympathetic to how Ms Eweida had, in fact, complied with the uniform code for around seven years but had then changed her practice. What was not acknowledged here was the freedom to change one's beliefs over the course of time [Article 9 (1)]. Unfortunately, while Article 9 recognises that people hold the freedom to change their beliefs, this Article had no automatic legal bearing in this case because there was no direct State interference. Convention rights incorporated into the Human Rights Act are only applicable to public authorities, not private companies. However, Article 9 may still be relevant if it can be found that the State failed to do what was required in protecting people's Article 9 rights within the private work sector.

## *The UK Government Submission and the Strasbourg Judgment in Eweida* [41]

Despite the Prime Minister's support for "the right of people to wear religious symbols at work",[42] the British Government in its official submission to the Strasbourg Court argued that Article 9 did not protect Ms Eweida, and that Strasbourg jurisprudence meant: 1) Not every act "motivated or inspired by religion or belief" was protected but only an "act of practice of a religion in a generally recognised form" (emphasis original). 2) The beliefs engaged had to be "intimately linked" to the act. (However, the Strasbourg Court stated, that a "sufficiently close and direct nexus" between an act and belief must be judged on the facts of each case.) 3) Only Article 9 manifestations involving "worship, teaching, practice or observance" were protected. The argument was that the wearing of the cross was not a *legally recognised* expression of Christian "worship" although such practice was, for Ms Eweida, an outward manifestation of faith, alongside the fact that the cross is recognised globally as the symbol of Christianity.

Yet the government contended there was "no suggestion that the wearing of a visible cross or crucifix was a generally recognised form of practicing" Christianity. The case involved "expression and not religious practice". If such acts were "practice" within the meaning of Article 9, there was still no interference because it was argued, if someone had voluntarily accepted work which did not accommodate their religious practice and, if other means were open to them to practice their religion "without undue hardship or inconvenience", their Article 9 rights were not violated: they were "free to resign", find alternative employment and "practice their religion unfettered outside their employment", thus guaranteeing their Article 9 rights. Ms Eweida argued before the Strasbourg Court that Christians should not be considered to have "waived" their rights by remaining in employment. The Court explained that given the importance of religious freedom in a democracy, the possibility of changing employment, owing to restrictions on religious freedom, could feature "in the overall balance" when deciding what was proportionate.

When responding to Ms Eweida's claim that adherents of other faiths were accommodated, the government argued that employers were "entitled" to treat expressions or acts motivated by religious beliefs (driven by personal choice) differently from "obligatory religious practices". Julian Rivers, a Professor of Jurisprudence, has written: "Christians have tended to lose out as compared with other religions, because Christian ethics is more individualistic and conscience-based, whereas other faiths tend to have 'mandatory' collective rules of behaviour."[43]

As noted earlier, Christianity has its commandments. But unlike Islam for example, where prayer is prescribed in its frequency, Christians are called to "pray continually"[44] and so the practice is advisory instead of mandatory. It is disturbing when judgments are made, defining the boundary lines of a believer's "worship" and its manifestation. The reality for Christians is not to have to demarcate artificial lines between "belief", "practice" and "worship"; instead these facets should work together holistically because

Christian faith, ultimately, is to live in a *relationship* with God. Therefore, it is odd to try subjecting this relationship to parameters chosen by lawyers or others who do not, presumably, hold to the faith. This position shows disrespect but also clearly demonstrates religious illiteracy.

A majority of the judges of the Strasbourg Court ruled Ms Eweida's right to wear a visible cross at work was legally protected. (A nurse, whose case was heard alongside Ms Eweida's, concerned the wearing of a visible crucifix at work but the court did not, on the specific facts, recognise her Article 9 rights had been violated.)

### *Lillian Ladele* [45]

Ms Ladele worked as a civil marriage registrar at the London Borough of Islington. She was threatened with dismissal and was found guilty of gross misconduct because her orthodox view of marriage meant she was unable to reconcile her Christian faith with facilitating the formation of same-sex civil partnerships, which came into legal effect in 2005, following the 2004 Civil Partnership Act. Her claims were ones of discrimination on grounds of religion, as well as harassment.

Her case held many legal merits, though other arguments were found to weaken her position. First, performing civil partnerships was not part of Ms Ladele's contract; her work began before the legal introduction of civil partnerships. She started as a statutory officer but, due to legal changes, she would eventually transfer to local authority control, giving Islington the power to dismiss her. In anticipation of these changes, Islington indeed threatened Ms Ladele with dismissal because the Council "would not accept her views" which contravened their *Dignity for All* policy, a Code given a distinct authority of its own.

Secondly, Islington was advised that the new civil

partnership law did not require all registrars to be designated to perform civil partnerships.[46] However, she was still designated as a civil partnership registrar without her consent.

Thirdly, her right to not be discriminated against in employment on grounds of religious belief was legally protected but this needed balancing against regulations prohibiting discrimination on grounds of sexual orientation in the provision of goods, facilities and services. As recognised by the courts and Islington Council, no suggestion was ever made that same-sex couples had been denied their legal rights. Ms Ladele had made adjustments to her work roster, designed to allow her willing colleagues to oversee civil partnerships. We can therefore conclude that what was being defended by Islington were not legal rights *per se* but the abstract ideological dogma underpinning them.

Fourthly, other registrars at Islington and other Councils were accommodated, within varying limits, to opt out from civil partnership work. Islington offered a temporary compromise, subject to review, in which Ms Ladele would participate in duties related to civil partnerships including signings, though where a ceremony was performed for the couple, she could opt out. She rejected this. In line with an increasing volume of cases coming to public attention, the Council's thinking here strongly reveals religious illiteracy. In choosing to abstain from participation in the formation of same-sex unions, Ms Ladele was holding true to her Christian belief that marriage was reserved for one man and one woman for life to the exclusion of all others, and that sexual relations outside marriage were sinful. Her conscience would not allow her to be complicit in actions, even when participation was limited to what the Council judged was peripheral to the civil partnership formation itself. To do so, she would have had to yield her conscience to the dictates of the Council.

Ms Ladele's counsel argued for accommodation by drawing an analogy with abortion law, in which people holding conscientious objections are protected from participation in most abortions. The Master of the Rolls, Lord Justice Dyson, in the Court of Appeal, argued that she was employed in a public job for a public authority and was required to perform a secular task. Yet, in the Strasbourg Court, her counsel reasoned it could not be assumed that accommodation would make it seem Islington was conferring public approval of her beliefs, because the State permitted doctors to opt-out from performing abortions, and this was not seen as approval of the doctors' views. Dissenting judges in the Strasbourg Court said: "instead it was a sign of tolerance on the part of the State."

Providing legal protection for an exercise of conscience should be integral to society's professed commitment to tolerance.

It seems Islington's overarching principle in determining the 'right' treatment of Ms Ladele was its own rule code, *Dignity for All*. This stated that "everyone should be treated fairly and without discrimination." This included not only customers with the right to "equal access" to services, but Islington would ensure fellow staff "experience fairness and equity of treatment in the workplace." Employees found in breach of this code faced a disciplinary offence. Interestingly, in this case, no one tried to suggest that the conscientious objection permitted by abortion law had undermined "equal access" to public services, which it does not. For almost 50 years, staff rosters on hospital wards in which abortions are performed have been managed, so that nurses and doctors are legally accommodated.

Two gay employees who were not "comfortable" with Ms Ladele's refusal to conduct civil partnerships wrote to complain to Council bosses, demanding prompt rectifying action, calling Ms Ladele's decision "an act of homophobia". They received a sympathetic reply and were informed "in confidencc" about how Ms Ladele's case was being handled in view of the law – all of this in breach of the Council's own Code of confidentiality.

The Council had not merely elevated the moral standing of its *Dignity for All* code, but its policy of 'fairness' was used to defend the sensitivities of one population group, while subsequently trying to eradicate the presence of diverse views and values within the workplace. Ultimately, it seemed to matter little what the law said against the Council's homespun morality code.

The Master of the Rolls, in a passing reference to Ms Ladele's Christian beliefs about marriage, made a surprising declaration: her objection to performing civil partnerships "was based on her view of marriage, which was not a core component of her religion." (In another case, the "core component" test was considered with reference to the issue of Sunday as a Sabbath day of rest).[47] The categorisation of Christian beliefs and questions of their overall importance is surely a matter for theologians and church leaders, not judges.[48] In fact, whatever phraseology we adopt – the judge's words are unhelpful here – it is undeniable that the institution of marriage, as the lifelong union of one man and one woman, for life, to the exclusion of all others, is a defining belief and practice within the Judaeo-Christian tradition. The explicit biblical teachings on marriage[49] clearly render the Bible and its body of teachings the core component of Christianity, without which knowledge of Christian beliefs would not exist.

In another unwarranted move into questions of Christian faith and doctrine, Lord Justice Dyson claimed that Islington's requirement for Ms Ladele to undertake civil partnerships "in no way prevented her from worshipping as she wished." He did not define what he meant by "worship" but his argument attempted to draw an unrealistic line between what she undertook at work and her freedom to worship. What does it mean "to worship" God? It is not, as so often thought, merely the singing of hymns or songs on Sundays. Such acts of worship are but examples of how Christians express their hearts to God. For the Christian, actual worship, if it is genuine and all-encompassing, inevitably involves every facet of living.[50]

The UK government's legal arguments made before the Strasbourg Court in Ms Ladele's case, including the ruling against her, are considered further below.

### *Gary McFarlane*[51]

Mr McFarlane was a counsellor dismissed for gross misconduct by Relate, a provider of relationship counselling services and sex therapy, for saying that he might have a conscientious objection to providing sex therapy to same-sex couples. He offered counselling to same-sex couples but the dispute revolved specifically around a hypothetical question regarding the provision of sex therapy for same-sex couples. He explained to Relate that should a situation arise over such a question, he would seek to work through the issue with his supervisors. Ultimately, this failed to satisfy Relate, who appealed to a Code of Ethics and Principles of Good Practice, to which all counsellors were said to be bound.[52] They were likewise expected to comply with Relate's equal opportunities policy, which was deemed to apply not merely to clients but counsellors too. It stated a commitment to ensuring no one was subjected to "less favourable treatment on the basis of personal or group characteristics, such as race, colour, age, culture, medical condition, sexual orientation, marital status, disability [or] socio-economic grouping."

'Religion' was noticeably absent from this list of personal or group features, clearly suggesting that religion was deemed as irrelevant as a personal or group characteristic worthy of *protection* under the equal opportunity policy.

Furthermore, while Relate declared itself "committed" to the "letter of the law" it also proudly claimed to hold to a "positive duty" designed to achieve equality for all of its employees. This begs two questions: how could Mr McFarlane's legal right to hold his beliefs, being protected by law,[53] be trumped by what was, in this case, the merely hypothetical rights of same-sex couples? And, by excluding religion from their list of equalities, and by committing themselves to a supposed "positive duty" to achieve an equality policy for their whole workforce, in which way was Mr McFarlane included and protected?

One central legal question hovering over this case was whether Relate's treatment of Mr McFarlane was a "proportionate means of achieving a legitimate aim."[54] Relate argued that its action was proportionate and justified and therefore it was not guilty of religious discrimination. The legal concept of proportionality should be capable of suggesting some sort of accommodation for both sides, since (actual or hypothetical) competing rights are being weighed against one another. In refusing any degree of accommodation, both Relate and the courts in this case, as in *Ladele*, had effectively rendered the application of proportionality of no value.

## 7.11   LORD CAREY'S INTERVENTION

In the Court of Appeal, Lord Carey (former Archbishop of Canterbury) felt "compelled to intervene" in support of Mr McFarlane. He threw a challenging spotlight on the stereotypical views held by senior Judges, of Christian sexual ethics being "discriminatory" and bigoted. He explained how the true Christian message of love does not demean anyone, believing the "highest development of human spirituality" was found in an "acceptance of Christ as saviour and adherence to Christian values" and this cannot be seen by England's courts as comparable to the "base and ignorant behaviour" suggested by crude stereotyping of Christians.

Christians voicing beliefs about traditional sexual ethics not unusually attract knee-jerk reactions of being "homophobic" and "bigoted". This brings to the fore an insight voiced by Jean-Paul Sartre, when he addressed the infighting in the French Communist Party: "the opponent is never answered; he is discredited." [55]

Lord Carey warned it is "but a short step from the dismissal of a sincere Christian from employment to a 'religious bar' to any employment by Christians." That clerics from the Church of England and other faiths have felt the necessity to intervene in judicial cases was, he said, "illuminative of a future civil unrest."

Lord Carey explained that how Christians were being viewed revealed a "lack of sensitivity to religious belief". This observation illustrates well the point made earlier about institutional religious illiteracy, which on the facts of the *McFarlane* and *Ladele* cases, exposed such illiteracy on numerous levels: Relate as a charity, Islington Council, the English courts, and as will be seen further below, UK government lawyers, through their various legal submissions to the Strasbourg Court, shared in this failing.

Lord Justice Laws in the Court of Appeal seems to have interpreted Lord Carey's comments to mean that a special plea was being made for protection of the "substance or content" of Christian beliefs, as opposed to legal protection of the right to hold and express Christian beliefs. Although Lord Carey had not asked for such special protection, Lord Justice Laws went on to speak of the "subjective opinion" upon which religious faith is based, being "incommunicable by any kind of proof or evidence." Legal protection of a "position held purely on religious grounds" was, he said, "irrational, as preferring the subjective over the objective."

It is questionable[56] when a judge – whose sole purpose is to sit on cases and interpret the law – makes sweeping agnostic pronouncements about the Christian faith. Millions of Christians throughout the world could easily testify to the importance of their faith, supported by the positively transforming impact it has on their lives. So it is difficult to see how classifying the nature of faith as purely "subjective" adds anything constructive to this debate, still less to the interpretation of the law.

Shortly before this case, Lord Justice Sedley in the same court suggested religion and belief are not "objective" characteristics, as are ethnicity, marital status and sexual orientation, a view far from categorical.[57] Sexual orientation includes the "subjective" domain of desires, while the status of marriage attracts the protection of the right to family life which includes the subjective experiences of its members. Crucially, these features are not treated in law as 'inferior' to those characteristics said to actually be subjective.

The claim that religious faith is purely "subjective" raises compelling questions about some of the potential subjective components of "sexual orientation". Sexual orientation categories (labels of "heterosexual", "homosexual", "gay" etc) are not neatly boxed concepts and may be determined by choices in self-designation. For example, people engaging in one-off or sporadic same-sex sexual activities may designate themselves as heterosexual; heterosexuals in prison environments sometimes participate in homosexual activities for the duration of their term; while for others, philosophical views or religious value parameters about identity render meaning to actual experiences.

In all these above senses, for a judge to deem religious faith as "subjective" while suggesting sexual orientation is simply "objective" is a flawed claim. It might be argued in the judge's defence that whereas people can change their religion, sexual orientation can never change. But this view – popular though it has apparently become – is not supported by the evidence.[58] As noted earlier, the rights and freedoms set out in Article 9 are fundamental in constituting a believer's identity, so deeming faith as 'subjective' is not helpful.

Lord Carey called for Mr McFarlane's case to be heard before a court constituted by judges holding "sensibility to religious issues". His request was not accepted but it was not asking for special treatment and could be likened, for example, to highly complex financial cases being referred to judges whose record or familiarity with niche areas of law allows them to connect with the case nuances more readily, which is likely to inspire greater confidence among the parties.

Likewise, those adjudicating on professional tribunals would be expected to have had "diversity training". Anything less would be judged as detrimental to providing a fair hearing for the accused. A genuine pluralism underpinning such diversity must therefore inevitably include knowledge and "literacy" about Christian beliefs and lifestyles in a form including less "popular" beliefs (which could have the potential to offend some people) such as marriage only involving opposite-sex couples.

According to Lord Justice Laws, Lord Carey's observations were "misplaced" because judges had never, he believed, equated a condemnation by some Christians of homosexuality for religious reasons, with homophobia or disrepute. It is contended here that the question is not what judges may or may not have said overtly of Christians, but it is the actual *effect* of their judgments against Christians manifesting their freedoms of belief and conscience that is the issue.

When this case was heard by the Strasbourg Court, no violation of Article 9 was found.


## 7.12 THE UK GOVERNMENT SUBMISSIONS AND STRASBOURG JUDGMENTS

### *Cases of Ladele and McFarlane*

The British government's legal submission in these cases[59] highlighted Strasbourg's recognition that "permitting and restricting manifestations of religious belief communicates important values for a society and has a significant symbolic, as well as practical, impact." It is hard to doubt that public messages, good or bad, are conveyed by the effect of court judgments.

The government argued that in cases involving incompatibility between a person's religious beliefs and their employment, their Article 9 rights were "guaranteed" because they were, in a similar vein of reasoning used against Ms Eweida, "free to resign" and "seek employment elsewhere". This effectively entails the view that those holding orthodox beliefs about marriage should not take part in professions in which they might manifest these beliefs.[60] This position is incompatible in a society priding itself on credentials of diversity and tolerance.

Mr McFarlane argued that like doctors with a legal right to opt-out from abortion on grounds of conscientious objection, he too should be offered such accommodation. The government argued, in general, that the "legitimate aim" of "equal access to services" rendered the question of accommodation "irrelevant to that aim", even while acknowledging the possibility of staff adjustments within the workplaces of both people.

Neither would Ms Ladele's argument about conscientious objection, as related to abortion, "assist" her. The UK authorities were free to legislate in this way but "religious belief does not justify discriminating on grounds of sexual orientation."

If staff rosters were amenable to adjustments so that services remained unrestricted, why should an *abstract* right connected to non-discrimination in Mr McFarlane's case, have been allowed to supersede an *actual* instance of an Article 9 right? It is difficult to see how protection of a right in the abstract can, in the words of the applicable law, be a "proportionate means of achieving a legitimate aim". The only answer appears to be that it was one of dogma.

### Religiously Motivated Acts and Questions of Religious Practice

The government contended that Article 9 protections were not relevant in *Ladele* and *McFarlane* since they were not manifestations of Article 9 ("worship, teaching, practice or observance"). As in *Eweida*, behaviour or expression motivated or inspired by religion or belief but which is not a religious act or practice of a "generally recognised form" was not protected, an argument recognised by a majority of the Strasbourg judges. This narrowly prescriptive interpretation is but more evidence of religious illiteracy, wrongly suggesting the 'actions' at issue were either *unrelated* to Christian morals, or the responses of both Christians were somehow *peripheral* to their faith. Acts or practices of a "generally recognised form" also suggest practices holding a majority currency among Christians. Here, we need to crucially distinguish between the orthodoxy of a religious principle from that of whether a minority or majority might follow it. These are two separate propositions and should not be linked, as if to suggest that "legitimacy" of practice is only established if the majority follow it.

We can say confidently that if "practice" for Christians is to be meaningful, it must include acts *and omissions*. Ms Ladele and Mr McFarlane were not merely appealing to conscience in the hope their positions could be accommodated. Both acted in accordance with long-established principles based on traditional Judaeo-Christian sexual ethics.[61] It sets a disturbing and dangerous precedent when government lawyers and the courts venture into the terrain of the application of Christian faith and doctrine, while demonstrating a stark level of ignorance about Christianity.

The Strasbourg judges held that there was no requirement for someone to show they were acting in fulfilment of a mandatory religious duty but this was not enough for the Court to recognise Article 9 protections in both cases. In *McFarlane*, the Court recognised the "severe sanction" of job loss and the subsequent grave consequences suffered by Mr McFarlane.

Article 14 was also used in both cases (in conjunction with Article 9) though unsuccessfully. It states that "enjoyment of the [Convention] rights and freedoms... shall be secured without discrimination on any ground such as sex, race, colour, language, religion, political or other opinion, national or social origin, association with a national minority, property, birth or other status." While the original Convention drafters did not mention "sexual orientation", "other status" is now interpreted to include this.

Two of the five dissenting Strasbourg judges noted how Islington Council's "blinkered political correctness" which favoured gay rights over fundamental human rights led to Ms Ladele's dismissal and that, as Article 9 (2) contained no restrictions on conscience, she had every right to act in accordance with her conscience.


## 7.13  CONSCIENTIOUS OBJECTION TO ABORTION

### Case of the Scottish Midwives [62]

Two practising Roman Catholic Scottish midwives found themselves at the centre of a legal case involving their statutory right to conscientiously object to participating in abortion "treatment". The Catholic position, like that of all orthodox-minded churches, holds that abortion is the murder of a child, who holds the right to life.  Procuring an abortion is still a crime[63] but what the 1967 Act did was to remove criminal liability if and when certain conditions are satisfied. It also provided medical personnel with the right to object to participating in abortion, unless it is necessary to save the life or to prevent grave permanent injury to the physical or mental health of the pregnant woman.[64]  It should be noted that the great majority of UK abortions do not involve saving the life of the pregnant woman.

The midwives, who had over twenty years of experience in the labour ward and helped to deliver about 10,000 babies,[65] began to experience problems when maternity services were reorganised, resulting in an increase in abortions carried out in the labour ard in which they worked as labour ward co-ordinators.  Their job duties potentially involved up to thirteen components, each of which were subjected to varying judicial scrutiny and questions of which ones attracted the conscience clause protection (section 4 (1)) and which ones did not.

Section 4 (1) provides that "no person shall be under any duty, whether by contract or by any statutory or other legal requirement, to participate in any treatment authorised by this Act to which he has a conscientious objection".

The two, central but merging, questions in this case were: 1) What does it mean "to participate in any treatment"? 2) What is the scope of the right to conscientiously object?

### "Participate in any treatment"

The conflict centred on the Health Board expecting the midwives to engage in work which involved delegating, supervising and supporting staff who were directly involved with patients undergoing abortions. The midwives first sought Judicial Review of this hospital decision on the basis that it was, among others things, *ultra vires* and contradicted the 1967 Act. The Lord Ordinary, Lady Smith, ruled that the conscience clause did not cover indirect involvement in abortion, saying: "Nothing they have to do as part of their duties terminates a woman's pregnancy. They are sufficiently removed from direct involvement..." to accommodate their beliefs. Furthermore, they "knowingly accepted that these duties were to be part of their job." In fact, the midwives had given notice to the hospital authorities about their conscientious objection, and according to the 1967 Act (section 4 (1)) they were never under a contractual duty to "participate".

According to the 1998 Human Rights Act, legislation must be read and interpreted in a way that is compatible with Convention Rights. Counsel for the midwives argued that Article 9 rights were relevant, alongside their right to opt-out under the 1967 Act. The Health Board, while not denying Article 9 rights were possibly engaged, also contended that if there was any interference with Article 9 rights, this was justified. However, as noted earlier, Article 9 contains no limit on the manifestation of conscience, but the implications of this fact were not addressed.

The case was appealed successfully before the Inner

House. Lady Dorrian who delivered the judgment, drawing on a House of Lords precedent,[66] held that "treatment" not only concerned those who directly undertook the abortion *per se* but also included those involved in the "whole process of treatment" leading to a termination. Furthermore, "treatment" included pre- and post-operative care.

In the UK Supreme Court, however, it was ruled that the midwives were expected to supervise and support staff who were involved in terminations. This ruling meant that there was an expectation to be complicit in actions believed to be morally repugnant, in effect, dismissing the midwives' pleas to exercise their consciences.

In Baroness Hale's judgment, agreed by the four other Justices, it was held that of the many duties midwives might ordinarily be tasked with, the right to exercise conscience would be more restricted than previously thought. So is *indirect participation* in the abortion process not legally protected?

### *What was Parliament's intention? Questions of Scope*
To help understand the meaning of a statute, an appeal to the 'mind' of Parliament helps ascertain the scope intended during the passage of the bill. During the parliamentary debates which led to the Abortion Act of 1967 one MP, in support of the bill, tried to reassure his opponents when he said the bill "requires no one to act in a way that his or her conscience forbids".[67] Dr David Owen, who was to become a Health Minister and Foreign Secretary, declared that nurses with religious objections who find abortion "distasteful" were free "to leave the operating theatre".[68] Both of these statements were clearly acknowledging that the law should respect conscience.

Norman Wylie, who had served briefly as Solicitor General before becoming an MP, and was later to become

Lord Advocate for Scotland, when moving an amendment of the conscience clause, made a further clarification:

*...I think that it was generally agreed in Committee...that a conscience Clause on the lines of Clause 4 was essential because, as one widened the scope in which the termination of a pregnancy ceased to be criminal, increasing pressures could be brought to bear on doctors and hospital staffs to perform an operation which might well be against their consciences. I understand that it was in the light of those considerations that the Clause was introduced.[69]*

Surprisingly, despite these clear parliamentary statements Lady Smith, in the initial hearing, insisted there was "no indication that Parliament intended a wider approach such as would cover all those who could in any way be said to have facilitated the giving of the treatment." And Baroness Hale asserted that the "narrow meaning is more likely to have been in the contemplation of Parliament when the Act was passed."

## Right of Conscience

In the appeal hearing, Lady Dorrian recognised: "It is in keeping with the reason for the exemption that the wide interpretation" of section 4 (1) is chosen, this being "consistent with the reasoning which allowed such an objection in the first place that it should extend to any involvement in the process of treatment, the object of which is to terminate a pregnancy." She explained that the person invoking their right to conscientious objection is not, according to the 1967 Act, under "any duty" to participate in "treatment" which is what the Act explicitly states, so it followed that the "management" of this right was a matter for the employee, not the employer.

These arguments, alongside the parliamentary references cited, reinforce the argument that the *raison d'etre* of the conscience clause was to afford individuals, whose conscience would be offended, the *freedom* not to have to participate in *any* "treatment", as the statute makes clear.[70] The plain ordinary meaning of "any" must inevitably give way to a wide, rather than narrow meaning.

In fact, Baroness Hale in the Supreme Court had noted how the "exercise of conscience is an internal matter which each person must work out", even though this fact was not enough, given her ruling, to allow an individual their right and freedom to exercise their conscience and have their employers respect that fact.

The Supreme Court, and the hospital authorities who rejected the midwives opt-out rights, further illustrate the institutional religious illiteracy at various levels.


7.14   QUESTIONS OF ACCOMMODATION

Before the Strasbourg judges in the cases studied earlier, several interveners offered submissions, including Lord Carey, Bishop Michael Nazir-Ali and the European Centre for Law and Justice, arguing that an analysis of proportionality should account for the possibility of accommodation of an individual's beliefs and practices, stressing that it was necessary for some compromise between competing rights in a "democratic and pluralistic society."[71] They further contended that as long as the practices of the believer did not pose any detriment to service provision or unduly affect an employer, religious practices should be permitted and protected in the workplace.

Interestingly, the Strasbourg judges stated that it is incompatible for a state to assess what are legitimate religious beliefs or the ways in which such beliefs are manifested, alongside its duty of neutrality and impartiality, when these beliefs are, among other things, serious and cohesive. The reality of UK State "neutrality" is, on the evidence, difficult to substantiate and thus remains more theoretical.

Baroness Hale, in a lecture to the Law Society of Ireland, posed the question: "So should we be developing, in both human rights and EU law, an explicit requirement upon the providers of employment, goods and services to make reasonable accommodation for the manifestation of religious and other beliefs?"[72]

It is submitted here that if competing rights are to be treated proportionately, legal decisions must have regard to reasonable accommodation, without which only one party is free to enjoy their rights. Laws and court decisions that reinforce the resulting injustice, either intentionally or through omissions, create *de facto* State sponsored discrimination.

Once it is recognised, in accordance with human rights law, that competing rights between different groups are at the fore, and to ensure that the manifestation of certain Article 9 rights are not *unreasonably* and *unjustly* confined to the private sphere, such freedoms should be respected by employers, and upheld by the courts by means of reasonable accommodation, so that Christians are protected from breaches of their fundamental freedoms.

## 7.15  SEEING BEYOND 'THE PROBLEMS'

The legal cases attracting public attention tell us nothing of those people who, in fear of job loss or possible social stigma, comply silently with politically correct demands at a cost to their fundamental freedoms.

Having identified 'the problems', what remedial responses might be suggested?

In-house employment codes of conduct, typically covering workplace "equality", should not readily interfere with such fundamental freedoms as expressions of religious belief and conscience. Increasingly, more cases emerge in which arguably no laws are broken; instead employers use their own homemade rule-book to sit in judgment over their employees, leaving a trail of legal and financial consequences.

The big 'elephant in the room' challenge for any government claiming faith-friendly credentials is whether legislation and public policy can, where fundamental freedoms are at issue, be enacted, or be better articulated than currently, to protect people from: 1) unreasonable employer interference with manifesting Article 9 rights; 2) court judgments effectively disregarding Article 9 rights without offering reasonable accommodation.

Finally, it is submitted that central government, with suitable legislative support, should pioneer and steer an educational strategy that positively includes religious literacy for *implementation* across the public and private sectors. Until then, more examples of institutional religious illiteracy are likely to continue surfacing. For any plan to be effective, it would need to match, for example, the unrelenting commitment and resources directed at the promotion of same-sex relationships as being an 'integral' part of modern 'diverse' Britain. To the extent that religious literacy does not feature as an integral part of diversity training, it suggests the rights of Christians seeking to exercise certain freedoms will continue to be placed at risk.

*Endnotes*

[1] *Religious Freedom in the World Report 2014*, published by Aid to the Church in Need. The report can only be accessed online: http://religion-freedom-report.org.uk/full-report/ [Accessed 1 March 2015].

[2] 'Christians are persecuted – but not in Britain', *Daily Telegraph*, Isabel Hardman, 25 October 2013, p. 28; 'Marginalised maybe,

but we aren't persecuted', *The Times*, Lord Harries (former Bishop of Oxford), 5 April 2010, p. 20. 'Persecution? Not here, says Williams', *Daily Telegraph*, 1 April 2010, p. 10. See also *Clearing the Ground Inquiry: Preliminary report into the freedoms of Christians in the UK,* Christians in Parliament, February 2012. This Inquiry reported that "Christians are experiencing marginalisation and discrimination in the UK, but they are not experiencing persecution." (p. 42) See also pp. 10, 23 and 46.

[3] *Clearing the Ground Inquiry*, pp. 23-24.

[4] Ibid., p. 25.

[5] Romans 13:1. (All biblical quotations are from the NIV, Hodder & Stoughton, 1992).

[6] Matthew 22:21.

[7] See 2 Corinthians 9:7.

[8] Acts 5: 29.

[9] Matthew 22:37-39.

[10] Letter, Rev Arun Arora, Director of Communications, Archbishops' Council, *Daily Telegraph*, 20 February 2015, p. 19.

[11] Isobel Hardman seemed to make a pertinent point when she wrote in the *Daily Telegraph*: "The centre of the faith is God in human form dying on a cross, not a sexual morality club." ('Christians are persecuted – but not in Britain', 25 October 2013, p. 28). But the support used for her argument that the church is not a "sexual morality club", draws on cases whose facts are based on incomplete and unsubstantiated reports. It is true that the epicentre of the faith is eclipsed by the standard biased news coverage depicting Christianity primarily in the context of what it prohibits, e.g. sexual relations outside the bonds of traditional marriage.

[12] In John 10:10, Jesus says: "… I have come that they may have life, and have it to the full."

[13] Kettel, Steve, *On the Public Discourse of Religion: An Analysis of Christianity in the United Kingdom,* Politics and Religion, p. 2, 2009; Religion and Politics Section of the American Political Science Association, published by the University of Warwick.

[14] See Romans 1:16.

[15] *Eweida and Others v The United Kingdom*, (2013), para. 79.

[16] Kettell, Steve, *On the Public Discourse of Religion: An Analysis of Christianity in the United Kingdom*, pp.14-15. Kettell, who is an Associate Professor in Politics and International Studies at

Warwick University questions the public role of Christianity as a moral adjudicator in the UK in so far, he believes, it "exempts itself from the evidentially-based standards and criteria that govern public life." (p.2). Kettell cites, among others, the Archbishop of York, Dr John Sentamu, who argues that "dogmatic assumptions also underpin non-religious worldviews – Marxism, Darwinism, Freudianism, capitalism, secularism, humanism and so on." (p.9) It is difficult to see how, for example, Marxist or humanist worldviews, would begin to meet the high evidence thresholds Kettell expects of Christianity, so he seems to refer to a successful counter-argument opposing his own position.

[17] *Fundamentalist World: The New Dark Age of Dogma*, Stuart Sim, Icon Books UK, 2005.

[18] For numerous secular examples of "fundamentalism", see *Fundamentalist World: The New Dark Age of Dogma*. We may also consider the case for showing how atheism and humanism, as adjudicating worldviews, hold to their own fixed ideological dogma, supported by debatable premises. The philosopher and leading gender theorist Judith Butler suggests that "secularism has a variety of forms and many of them involve forms of absolutism and dogmatism that are surely as problematic as those that rely on religious dogma." (*Sexual Politics, torture, and secular time*, The British Journal of Sociology, Volume 59, Issue 1, p.13, London School of Economics and Political Science, 2008).

[19] *The Meaning of Things: Applying Philosophy to Life*, London: Phoenix, 2002, p. 9.

[20] Butler, Eamonn, *The Rotten State of Britain: Who is Causing the Crisis and How to Solve it*, Gibson Square, London, 2009, p. 277.

[21] 'Believe it or not, the bigots are dying out', Emma Duncan, *The Times*, 28 October 2014, p 24.

[22] Independent schools must actively promote "British values" which, among other things, include "mutual respect and tolerance of those with different faiths and beliefs". See The Education (Independent School Standards) (England) (Amendment) Regulations 2014. These "British values" have also been applied to state schools and have been held by government ministers to define modern citizenship in Britain.

[23] A good introduction to the type of cases becoming more common can be found in: *Christians in the Firing Line*, Dr Richard Scott,

Wilberforce Publications, 2013; *Marginalising Christians: Instances of Christians being sidelined in modern Britain*, The Christian Institute, Newcastle upon Tyne, 2009.

[24] *Case of Eweida and Others v The United Kingdom*, para. 79.

[25] Christians should 'leave their beliefs at home or get another job', *Daily Telegraph*, 4 September 2012.

[26] Bingham, Tom, *The Rule of Law*, Penguin Books, 2011, pp 76-77.

[27] See the right to Freedom of Expression (Article 10) of the Human Rights Act 1998, which includes "freedom to hold opinions and to receive and impart information and ideas without interference by public authority." Like the right to freedom of belief and religion, Article 10 is a qualified right subject to possible limitations.

[28] Joint Partly Dissenting Opinion of Judges Vučinić and De Gaetano, para. 2, in *Eweida and Others v The United Kindgdom*, (2013).

[29] Cited in *What Price Liberty? How Freedom was won and is being lost*, Ben Wilson, Faber and Faber, 2009, p. 390 (quoted from the 1945 Preface to *Animal Farm*).

[30] 'Britain being taken over by 'militant secularists', *Daily Telegraph*, 14 February 2012, p. 1; also commentary from Baroness Warsi, the first British Muslim cabinet minister (p.2), 'We stand side by side with the Pope in fighting for faith.'

[31] 'Anglicans and atheists, unite against intolerance', *The Times*, 21 July 2014.

[32] Manifesto for Secularism, 14 October 2014. www.petertatchellfoundation.org/religion/manifesto-secularism-against-religious-right [Accessed 1 March 2015].

[33] 'Christians more militant than Muslims, says equality chief', *Daily Mail*, 20 June 2011, p. 17.

[34] 'Religion seen an 'oddity' by ministers, Archbishop says', 12 December 2009. http://news.bbc.co.uk/1/hi/uk/8409310.stm [Accessed 1 March 2015].

[35] *National Secular Society and Clive Bone v Bideford Town Council* [2012] EWHC 175 Admin.

[36] See *Eweida and British Airways PLC*, Employment Appeal Tribunal, UKEAT/0123/08/LA; *Eweida and British Airways PLC*, Court of Appeal, [2010] EWCA Civ 80 and *Eweida and Others v The United Kingdom*, Application nos. 48420/10, 59842/10, 51671/10 and 36516/10 (Judgment, 15 January 2013).

[37] 'BA uniform review after cross row', BBC, 24 November 2006. http://news.bbc.co.uk/1/hi/england/london/6181746.stm [Accessed 1 March 2015].

[38] 1 Corinthians 15:17.

[39] 'Top European Court to decide if wearing the cross is a right', *Catholic Herald*, March 16 2012, p.1.

[40] The relevant law used was the Employment Equality (Religion or Belief) Regulations 2003, since replaced by the Equality Act 2010.

[41] 1) Nadia Eweida 2) Shirley Chaplin v United Kingdom, Respondent's Observations, Foreign and Commonwealth Office, 14 October 2011.

[42] Hansard, 11 July 2012, Col 307.

[43] *Uniformity or mutuality? The new equality law in Christian perspective*, Cambridge Papers, Vol. 20, No. 3, p. 4, Sept 2011 (Jubilee Centre).

[44] 1 Thessalonians, 5: 17.

[45] Her case was heard by an Employment Tribunal in 2008 (Case Number: 2203694/2007) in which her claims succeeded. An Employment Appeal Tribunal reversed this [2008] UKEAT 0453 08 1912. The case progressed to the Court of Appeal [2009] EWCA Civ 1357, being heard by the Master of the Rolls, finally culminating at the Strasbourg Court (*Eweida and Others v The United Kingdom*, Judgment delivered, 15 January 2013).

[46] See Civil Partnership Act 2004, section 29 (2).

[47] See *Mba v London Borough of Merton* [2013] EWCA Civ.

[48] In *R (Williamson) v Secretary of State for Education and Employment [2005] 2 AC 246*, Lord Nicholls in the House of Lords held it was not for the court to enquire into the 'validity' of a belief (see para. 22 for his qualifying remarks).

[49] In one of the most defining biblical verses conveying the importance of marriage for Christians, in Matthew 19:4, Jesus quoted from the book of Genesis: "Haven't you read," he replied, "that at the beginning the Creator 'made them male and female', and said, 'For this reason a man will leave his father and mother and be united to his wife, and the two will become one flesh'? So they are no longer two, but one. Therefore what God has joined together, let man not separate." It is also noteworthy that in Roman Catholic teaching, marriage is one of the seven sacraments. See the *Catechism of the Catholic Church*.

[50] Jesus does not stipulate boundary lines within which Christians are called to worship God. On the contrary, he explains (Mark 12:30) the greatest commandment is to love God with all one's heart, soul, mind and strength; thus, the commandment is simultaneously an invitation and imperative, and can be both broad and narrow in its application. In Romans 12:1-2, the practical expression of worship is given further explanation: "Therefore, I urge you, brothers, in view of God's mercy, to offer your bodies as living sacrifices, holy and pleasing to God – this is your spiritual act of worship. Do not conform any longer to the pattern of this world, but be transformed by the renewing of your mind. Then you will be able to test and approve what God's will is – his good, pleasing and perfect will."

[51] Gary McFarlane's case was first heard at an Employment Tribunal in 2008, Case No. 1401179/08, followed by an Employment Appeal Tribunal in 2009 (UKEAT/0106/09/DA), then at the Court of Appeal [2010] EWCA Civ 880 and finally heard in the European Court of Human Rights, *Case of Eweida and Others v The United Kingdom*, 15 January 2013.

[52] The Code was held by the British Association for Sexual and Relationship Therapy. It included the right to respecting the "autonomy and ultimate right to self-determination of clients and of others with whom clients may be involved. It is not appropriate for the therapist to impose a particular set of standards, values or ideals upon clients." What stands out here is that in the name of apparent neutrality, counsellors must appear to exercise impartiality in relation to their clients, a standard Relate was noticeably absent in applying towards one of its employees. Second, therapists were expected to be aware of their prejudices in a way that might affect the therapeutic relationship. Again, this ideal was only expected to be practised by counsellors toward their clients. Is it not reasonable to expect the counselling profession to be equally sensitive to the personal circumstances of its counsellors, so that their rights are also respected?

[53] The two areas of legislation used in support of Mr McFarlane were: the Employment Equality (Religion or Belief) Regulations 2003, since replaced by the Equality Act 2010, and Article 9 of the Human Rights Act 1998. Article 14 was also used before the Strasbourg Court.

[54] This test was drawn directly from the Employment Equality (Religion or Belief) Regulations 2003.

[55] Cited by Stuart Sim in *Fundamentalist World*, p. 162.

[56] Christianity, essentially a *personal faith* in Jesus Christ as Lord, is not without a foundation in reason and evidences. The subject of apologetics appeals to argument and evidences (including historical fact) in defence of the Christian faith. See, for example, *The Case for Christ: A Journalist's Personal Investigation of the Evidence for Jesus*, Lee Strobel, Zondervan: Grand Rapids, Michigan (1998); *The New Evidence That Demands a Verdict*, by Josh McDowell, Authentic Media, Milton Keynes (2012).

[57] Lord Justice Sedley in the Court of Appeal suggested that religion and belief are "matters of choice" and are not "objective" characteristics like "age, disability, gender reassignment, marriage, civil partnership, race…sex and sexual orientation." (*Eweida and British Airways PLC* [2010] EWCA Civ 80, para 40). But this conclusion is far from obvious. For example, is it not generally a matter of choice when people make a personal judgement about how they want their ethnic status to be classified? In cases of mixed ethnicity, people are deemed competent to choose their racial designation and in this sense, the designation is not evidently predictable by others in an "objective" sense. Gender reassignment is also a choice, albeit one influenced by internal conflicts.

[58] See 'Can Some Gay Men and Lesbians Change Their Sexual Orientation? 200 Participants Reporting a Change from Homosexual to Heterosexual Orientation', Robert Spitzer, October 2003, Archives of Sexual Behavior. Vol., 32, No. 5, 403-417; 'Ex-Gays? A Longitudinal Study of Religiously Mediated Change in Sexual Orientation', Stanton L. Jones and Mark Yarhouse, 2007, Illinois: IVP Academic, InterVarsityPress.

[59] (1) Lillian Ladele 2) Gary McFarlane v United Kingdom, Observations of the Government of the United Kingdom, Foreign and Commonwealth Office, 14 October 2011.

[60] Consider the Public Sector Equality Duty, Equality Act 2010, especially section 149, which places compliance obligations on public authorities and others exercising public functions, in a way that "may involve treating some persons more favourably than others", subject to the Equality Act 2010. The potential effect of this law means partial treatment may be shown to a 'favoured'

group over another whose values are disliked.

[61] Contrary to the fashions of our time, sexual relations are, according to traditional Christian teaching, designed solely for married, opposite-sex couples. Sexual activity outside of the bonds of marriage is deemed sinful. It is understandable and should be no surprise when Christians holding to this view act according to their consciences, by refraining from all and any acts that could be seen to approve, facilitate or support, the acts of others which are incompatible with Christian teaching. (Romans 1:32)

[62] An application for Judicial Review was heard in 2012 [2012] CSOH 32, followed by a hearing before the Inner House, Court of Session [2013] CSIH 36 and culminating in the UK Supreme Court: [2014] UKSC 68. The parties were Greater Glasgow and Clyde Health Board and the midwives, Mary Doogan and Concepta Wood.

[63] See Offences Against the Person Act 1861, sections 58 and 59.

[64] See section 4 (2) of the Abortion Act 1967.

[65] *Pro-Life Times*, (SPUC) February 2015, p. 1.

[66] *Royal College of Nursing* v *Department of Health and Social Security* 1981 AC 800.

[67] Edward Lyons, Hansard, HC Deb 22 July 1966, vol 732, col 1090.

[68] Ibid., cols 1113-1114.

[69] Hansard, HC Deb, 13 July 1967, vol 750, col 1313.

[70] This is subject to section 4 (2).

[71] *Eweida and Others v The United Kingdom*, para 78.

[72] Annual Human Rights Lecture, *Freedom of Religion and Belief*, Law Society of Ireland, 13 June 2014.

Chapter Eight

# THE CLASH OF MORALITIES: PERSONAL REFLECTION AND THE LAW OF RELIGIOUS LIBERTY

Paul Diamond

## 8.1 INTRODUCTION

January 2013 marked a watershed moment for British Christians who wish to express their faith at work and in the public space. In that month the European Court of Human Rights (ECHR) gave judgment on a number of cases related to alleged religious discrimination against Christians, bringing a wider European opinion to what has, in recent years, been a controversial subject in English Law. The judgments included a victory for Nadia Eweida,[1] an employee of British Airways. This article examines her case in detail.

The judgments from the ECHR area represent a fitting moment to take stock; to reflect on the changing nature of religious liberty in the United Kingdom, the animus toward the Christian faith and the response in the current climate.

It is important to place legal cases in societal context. Since early in the twentieth century, the United Kingdom has moved away from a moral framework represented and informed by the Christian faith and of wider Judaeo-Christian values. These ethics have now been replaced by an aggressive secularism and further challenged by the arrival of new religions and faiths.

## 8.2  A PERSONAL INDULGENCE

It takes me by surprise to find myself as one of the leading barristers in the law of religious liberty precisely because it was my objective as far back as 1982 when I began my study of law.  It is a rare privilege to fulfil one's ambitions. That is not to say that the specialising in such a field was simple; when I began my focus in about 1988 most of my contemporaries thought that I had lost touch with reality.

In 1988 Margaret Thatcher was Prime Minister, the United Kingdom was firmly under the rule of law and society was very much stronger than today.  The issues of the day were the power of organised labour, the trade union movement and the introduction of free market economics.  Those days seem to look so peaceable from today's vantage points.

My first opportunity occurred in the 1980s when I was appointed barrister to the *Keep Sunday Special Campaign*. The then Prime Minister, Mrs Thatcher, had commissioned the Auld Report[2] which recommended the introduction of Sunday trading.  The Government Bill introduced in April 1986 was defeated by 14 votes becoming only the second Government defeat that century.  Thereafter a number of legal cases took place when a number of DIY retailers challenged our Sunday trading law as contrary to European Community law as a *'quantitative restriction'* on the free movement of goods.[3]  Any restrictions on trade had to be justified under the *rule of reason*[4] and the then novel application of *socio cultural norms*.  I learned a unique skill and mix of European law, labour law and constitutional law which has stood the test of time.

One of the first acts of the new Labour Government under Tony Blair in 1997 was to introduce the Human Rights Act 1998 which incorporated the European Convention on Human Rights and Fundamental Freedoms (1950) into domestic law.[5]  This Act was controversial because a number of wise heads in the British Parliament assessed the political narrative of the human rights agenda. Baroness Young[6] instructed me as a young barrister to advise her on the impact of the Convention on religious rights. I thought up various examples of potential concerning situations which other Parliamentarians were informed about and Baroness Young sought amendments to the Human Rights Act.

My scenarios were ridiculed by the Government and their powerful supporters but I held my ground on my modest suggestions. If I had postulated *then* that it would be necessary to defend the rights of Christians to wear a cross or of a Christian family to foster a child in a matter of years, I myself would not have believed it and the proponents would have used any such postulation as a sign of scaremongering.


8.3 BACKGROUND

The United Kingdom has no written Constitution; the sovereignty of Parliament is the overarching legal principle. The European Convention on Human Rights and Fundamental Freedoms (1950) was ratified by the United Kingdom in 1953. As the United Kingdom was a dualist State[7] it was only incorporated into domestic law in 2000 by the Human Rights Act 1998. The United Kingdom entered the European Union in 1973 and the European Communities Act 1972 gives primacy to Union law over national law.

Legal practice in the United Kingdom is currently premised on a complex overlapping system of national law, EU law and Convention law; all of these sources of law assisted by the *'soft law'* of international organisations such as the *United Nations*.

## 8.4 HARRY HAMMOND – THE LAST ENGLISH MARTYR?

On a Saturday afternoon in October of 2001, Mr Hammond went into Bournemouth city centre carrying a placard which read: *Jesus Gives Peace, Jesus is Alive, Stop Immorality, Stop Homosexuality, Stop Lesbianism, Jesus is Lord.*

Mr Hammond was no stranger to controversy. Based on past experience he had covered up his placard on his bus journey in to the centre of the town so that he did not cause a disturbance.

Once he had set up his placard and started to speak a crowd surrounded him, pushed him to the ground, threw water and soil at him and pulled down his sign. This incident on its own might have warranted some comment, but it is what happened next that has significant implications for religious adherents, and with hindsight represented a foretaste of what was to come.

The police arrived at the scene, noted that Mr Hammond had been assaulted, and rather than arrest any of those who attacked him, arrested Mr Hammond on the grounds that he had, in effect, incited the attack on himself. The legislation that they used to effect an arrest was Section 5 of the Public Order Act 1986 which states that:

*A person is guilty of an offense if he displays any writing, sign or other visible representation which is threatening, abusive or insulting, within the hearing or sight of a person likely to be caused harassment, alarm or distress thereby.*[8]

At the trial the police conceded that they were unsure whether they should protect Mr Hammond or arrest him, and indeed they may well have believed that in arresting him they were offering him some protection. Nevertheless Mr Hammond was charged and the case was brought to trial; he was found guilty and ordered to pay fines and costs totalling £695.

After his conviction Mr Hammond was hospitalised and died shortly thereafter.

A posthumous appeal was launched in the High Court in 2004. The court acknowledged that Mr Hammond should have the right to freedom of religion including the freedom to express his beliefs, but ruled that he had acted unreasonably in holding up a sign he knew to be offensive.[9] In their judgment the Justices asserted that the content of the message on Mr Hammond's placard was insulting to the gay community and that it was not reasonable in law for Mr Hammond to show this placard. In their judgment, specifically relating to the findings of the lower court, they said:

*Accordingly, not without hesitation, I have reached the conclusion that it was open to the justices to reach the conclusion that they did as to the fact that these words on the sign were, in fact, insulting.*[10]

Accordingly the appeal failed, and a further appeal to the European Court of Human Rights was dismissed. The case provoked a national debate at the time, with a number of social commentators defending Mr Hammond's right to free speech.

One of the most unlikely defenders of Mr Hammond's rights was Peter Tatchell, a well-known gay rights activist in the UK. In a letter to The Spectator Mr Tatchell asserted:

*His [Mr Hammond's] placard was offensive to gay people; that is not, however, a legitimate reason to suppress his right to protest and turn him into a criminal. Freedom of speech is so precious that it must be defended, even when we disagree with the sentiments expressed. Other than direct incitements to violence, there is no justification for criminalising words and opinions. If Mr Hammond appeals, I would gladly testify in favour of his conviction being overturned.*[11]

It would seem that a veteran gay rights activist has more

human understanding and appreciation of the importance of freedom of speech, even when the expression of that 'speech' is offensive to him, than the Divisional Court.

The legislation used to arrest Mr Hammond had its roots in the Public Order Act of 1936, passed to counter the threat of Oswald Mosley's Black Shirts who were at the time planning to march through the East End of London. An Act to defend the Jewish community was used to prosecute an old man. The targeting of 'homophobic' offences against a religious preacher was done on executive directive that required no Parliamentary debate and the concept of inciting violence against oneself by the exercise of free speech rights is now a facet of modern European society. This was a depressing sign of the new primitivism that was evolving in a secular human rights agenda.


## 8.5  THE OFFENCE OF THE CROSS

In 2003, a lady called Nadia Eweida came to my Chambers to discuss a number of issues. She raised a number of concerns about the practices of *British Airways* which, in particular, concerned the privileging of other religions such as Islam over Christianity. In particular, *British Airways* permitted the wearing of the *hijab, turban* and *Hindu shikha*,[12] but banned the wearing of the Christian cross as this was classified as jewellery.[13]

In 2006, Ms Eweida put on her cross and was immediately sent home without pay. And there began one of Britain's best known cases. The case was hard fought with *British Airways* adopting[14] a very inflexible position. There was extensive media coverage in which *British Airways* was ridiculed and subject to criticism, including from the then Prime Minister, Tony Blair. They continued to fight the case despite the fact that in February 2007 they amended their uniform policy to permit the wearing of a cross and Star of David.[15]

One of the difficulties in articulating a case on behalf of the religious adherent is that the United Kingdom has a very weak tradition of *positive* human rights. Article 9 of the European Convention protects religious liberty and the Human Rights Act 1998 has incorporated this provision into domestic law. However, our judges have taken a very poor view of religious rights from Strasbourg and have preferred to rely on domestic anti discrimination law.[16]

As held by Lord Bingham, who commented in the context of Article 9 that:

*The Strasbourg institutions have not been at all ready to find an interference with the right to manifest religious belief in practice or observance where a person has voluntarily accepted an employment or role which does not accommodate that practice or observance and there are other means open to the person to practise or observe his or her religion without undue hardship or inconvenience".[17]*

Thus, when Ms Eweida appeared before the national courts, short shrift was given to her rights of religious liberty under Article 9. Thus, it was necessary to show discrimination against Christians, rather than the very obvious point that the Christian faith was disrespected by one of Britain's largest companies.

Employment Judge Lewis dismissed the claim at first level holding:

*We find that the Respondent would have treated identically*[18]...

- *An adherent of any non Christian faith, or of no faith displaying a Cross for cosmetic ... reasons*
- *An adherent of a faith other than Christianity wearing a symbol ... round the neck*
- *An employee wearing a visible silver necklace...*

In short, there was *no* discrimination because if a Muslim

had decided to wear a cross the adherent of the Islamic faith would have been treated exactly the same and sent home. One can hear the reader cry: 'But Muslims and Sikhs don't want to wear a cross and Christians don't want to wear a hijab or turban'. Such common sense was absent in this case.

On appeal, Lord Justice Sedley criticised the entire case as pursuing a 'sectarian agenda' as part of a strategy which involved a rejection of an 'open offer to settle the claim on generous terms'; and he appeared to support a 'blanket ban' on all religious rights in the workplace.[19] This approach is clearly wrong as Ms. Eweida was fully entitled to pursue her claim to establish a violation of her Convention Right.

The Court of Appeal further held that in order to establish indirect discrimination, disparate impact had to be established against a group of people; this is now known as 'Group Disadvantage'. Thus, in Ms. Eweida's case, there was found to be insufficient evidence that Christians felt strongly about the wearing of the cross and 'Group Disadvantage' was not established.

This decision exemplifies the anti-discrimination approach, rather than the religious liberty approach. In total, 13 British judges (including in the Supreme Court) came up with a variety of legal justifications as to why the cross was unprotected; the Judiciary set the legal threshold so high that it was close to impossible to prevail in such a case: the exact meaning of the concept of 'Group Disadvantage' was so vague and difficult to establish, the Courts had effectively prevented any recognition of a right to wear a cross.

The Judiciary was brought into disrepute by the Judiciary; and ironically after every defeat the case went to a higher and more important level.

Ms. Eweida went to the European Court of Human Rights in Strasbourg (along with nurse Shirley Chaplin)[20] and she prevailed. The judgment of the European Court of Human Rights in *Eweida & Others v United Kingdom*[21] was extremely important as it recognised the importance of religious freedom in Article 9 of the Convention (the religious liberty approach); and the views of British judges that Article 9 was of no consequence was erroneous. This case has opened the door to an expanded concept of religious liberty of growing benefit to religious adherents.

## 8.6 THE WAR ON CHRISTIAN CONSCIENCE AND MORALS

### *Example of Mr McFarlane and Ms Ladele*

The case of *McFarlane v United Kingdom* and its sister case *Ladele v United Kingdom* raised the issue of religious conscience.

Gary McFarlane was a Relate Counsellor in Bristol; he was good at his work and was progressing in the organisation. Gary had given relationship counselling to two same sex couples but he was uncertain about giving directive sexual therapy to a same sex couple because of his Christian faith.

His employer regarded such hesitation as contrary to Relate's Equality Policy; some fellow counsellors raised the usual cry of 'homophobia'. Mr McFarlane was required by his employer to, in effect, renounce his Christian views as a condition of employment; namely that he would set aside his Christian conscience whenever it conflicted with an instruction from the employer. He did not know himself what his view was, and he had never disobeyed a lawful instruction, declined a client or 'discriminated'.

He had committed a pure *thought crime*. He was dismissed for the holding of the view that marriage is between a man and woman and the putative belief that giving directive sexual counselling to a same sex couple 'could' violate his religious beliefs.

As Relate does couple counselling, people present themselves on arrival as couples in a relationship, so same-sex couples could have been directed to another counsellor without difficulty (after all, who would want a person who finds a same-sex relationship problematic?). Mr McFarlane was dismissed for *gross misconduct* on principle. *Gross misconduct* is the more serious form of employee misbehaviour usually associated with theft, violence or drunkenness.

Ms Ladele was a Christian like Gary McFarlane and she didn't want to participate in same-sex civil partnership ceremonies in her work as a Marriage Registrar at Islington Borough Council. Again, she could have been accommodated as other staff members could have been allocated to the needs of the small number of same-sex couples, but was forced to resign as her employer insisted that she was acting in a discriminatory fashion.

The following dialogue in the two cases illuminates the issues in conflict.

In the Court of Appeal, Lord Neuberger held in *Ladele v Islington LBC*[22]

*[52] However, even assuming that argument could be run here, it appears to me that the fact that Ms Ladele's refusal to perform civil partnerships was based on her religious view of marriage could not justify the conclusion that Islington should not be allowed to implement its aim to the full, namely that all registrars should perform civil partnerships as part of its Dignity for All policy. Ms Ladele was employed in a public job and was working for a public authority; she was being required to perform a purely secular task, which was being treated as part of her job; Ms Ladele's refusal to perform that task involved discriminating*

*against gay people in the course of that job; she was being asked to perform the task because of Islington's Dignity for All policy, whose laudable aim was to avoid, or at least minimise, discrimination both among Islington's employees, and as between Islington (and its employees) and those in the community they served; Ms Ladele's refusal was causing offence to at least two of her gay colleagues; Ms Ladele's objection was based on her view of marriage, which was not a core part of her religion; and Islington's requirement in no way prevented her from worshipping as she wished.*

And in paragraph [73]–

*however much sympathy one may have with someone such as Ms Ladele, who is faced with choosing between giving up a post she plainly appreciates or officiating at events which she considers to be contrary to her religious beliefs, the legislature has decided that the requirements of a modern liberal democracy, such as the United Kingdom, include outlawing discrimination in the provision of goods, facilities and services on grounds of sexual orientation, subject only to very limited exceptions.*

Ms Ladele was found to have *discriminated against homosexuals*, she could still worship (not practise her religion) and her views on marriage were not a core part of her religion (a secular court ruling on religious truth). To make matters worse, Lord Neuberger held that the comparator for discrimination purposes was a person who objected to same-sex marriage without a religious belief (who could be a bigot).

This judgment by Lord Neuberger is both base and crude which shows a total lack of understanding of religious belief and has played a significant role in the undermining of the United Kingdom as a civilised country. Of particular concern was the forced conformity and disrespect for conscience.

Mr McFarlane's case was listed in the Court of Appeal

shortly after this case; and this binding[23] decision needed to be addressed. Lord Carey, the former Archbishop of Canterbury came to the rescue. He filed a seminal Witness Statement on behalf of Mr McFarlane that will be seen by history as significant. He said:

*The comparison of a Christian, in effect, with a 'bigot' (i.e. a person with an irrational dislike to homosexuals) begs further questions. It is further evidence of a disparaging attitude to the Christian faith and its values. In my view, the highest development of human spirituality is acceptance of Christ as saviour and adherence to Christian values. This cannot be seen by the Courts of this land as comparable to base and ignorant behaviour. My heart is in anguish at the spiritual state of this country.*

*It is, of course, but a short step from the dismissal of a sincere Christian from employment to a 'religious bar' to any employment by Christians. If Christian views on sexual ethics can be described as 'discriminatory', such views cannot be 'worthy of respect in a democratic society'. An employer could dismiss a Christian, refuse to employ a Christian and actively undermine Christian beliefs. I believe that further Judicial decisions are likely to end up at this point and this is why I believe it is necessary to intervene now.*

Lord Carey's view is of course prophetic, and accurate, and we must be grateful that he intervened so forcefully when he did. Lord Justice Laws dismissed Mr McFarlane's case which proceeded to the European Court of Human Rights.

Importantly, the European Court of Human Rights recognised the Religious Rights of both Mr McFarlane and Ms Ladele but declined to intervene with the decision of the United Kingdom because of the sensitivity of the subject matter of the conflicting rights under the doctrine of the *'margin of appreciation'*.

## Example of Mr and Mrs Johns

Shortly after this case, in *R (Johns) v Derby City Council*[24] a Christian couple were prevented from fostering because of their Christian views on homosexuality. Mr and Mrs Johns were a stable and loving couple with a spare room in their house. They wanted to assist another couple in need so they asked the local council if they could foster a 5 year old child (or other young child) for respite care. Respite care is a form of temporary relief for parents who care for a mentally or physically disabled child (who might otherwise be in an institution). Thus, the Johns sought a *difficult* child for the weekend to enable another couple (perhaps at the end of their tether) to have some time off together.

The social workers noted in interview that the Johns were Christians and questions were asked about their views on homosexuality. Mrs Johns wondered why this question was relevant for a 5 year old, but said she would love any child. Mr Johns said he would *'gently turn'* the child away from homosexuality. And the scene was set for court action. The social services recognised that Mr and Mrs Johns would have provided a good home for any child but for their Christian views.

Lord Justice Munby gave judgment in vitriolic terms describing my argument as a *'travesty of reality'*. Whilst it is always embarassing to focus on criticism of oneself, it is important to report what he thought should not have been said in Court:

*[33] Thus Mr Diamond's skeleton argument opens with these words, "This case raises profound issues on the question of religious freedom and whether Christians (or Jews and Muslims) can partake in the grant of 'benefits' by the State, or whether they have a second class status"* (emphasis in original). *He continues, "The advancement of*

*same sex rights is beginning to be seen as a threat to religious liberty". He asserts that "something is very wrong with the legal, moral and ethical compass of our country" and that "Gay rights advocates construe religious protection down to vanishing point." He submits that the State "should not use its coercive powers to de-legitimise Christian belief." He asserts that what he calls the modern British State is "ill suited to serve as an ethical authority" and complains that it "is seeking to force Christian believers 'into the closet'." He identifies the issue before the court as being "whether a Christian couple are 'fit and proper persons' (Counsel's use of phrase) to foster (and, by implication, to adopt) by reason of their faith" and "whether Christian (and Jewish and Muslim) views on sexual ethics are worthy of respect in a democratic society." The manner in which he chooses to frame the argument is further illustrated by his submissions that what is here being contended for is "a blanket denial on all prospective Christian foster parents in the United Kingdom", indeed "a blanket ban against all persons of faith", an "irrebutable presumption that no Christian (or faith adherent) can provide a suitable home to a child in need of a temporary placement", that "the denial of State benefits to those who believe homosexuality is a 'sin' must be premised on the basis that such beliefs are contrary to established public policy" and that what is being said amounts to this, that "the majority of world religions [are] deemed to have a belief system that could be described as bigotry or discriminatory because of a code of sexual ethics that some people disagree with."*

*It is hard to know where to start with this travesty of the reality…*

Whilst I might put some of my submissions differently to how I made them some years ago, I hope the reader can see the force of my submissions whether they disagree or not; and, as Counsel, I must present the case without fear or favour. What was said, needed to be said!

It is also instructive to note that the submissions of my opponent on behalf of the Equality and Human Rights Commission said:

*In addition to the harm that it may cause children in their care, approving foster carers who express antipathy to, or disapproval of, homosexuality and same sex relationships militates against the promotion of sexual orientation equality more generally, providing state sanction as it would to views that are inimical to such equality. This is in conflict with the aspirations of anti discrimination and human rights law, and carries the real risk that the child in the care of such a foster carer will become <u>infected</u> with, or affected by, such views (underlining added).*

Thus, my opponent's submission was not only that Judaeo Christian views on sexual ethics were in conflict with human rights law, but a child could be '*infected*' with such views. Imagine if Counsel had made the submission that a child could be '*infected*' with Islamic values, or homosexual viewpoints: I objected in open court and was brushed off – only to receive the judgment above. It is no exaggeration to say that appearing in some of these cases can be an ordeal.

The court also noted that:

*If children, whether they are known to be homosexuals or not, are placed with carers who, in the language used by way of description in Ms Monaghan's written submissions, evince an antipathy, objection to or disapproval of, homosexuality and same-sex relationships, there may well be a conflict with the local authority's duty to "safeguard and promote" the "welfare" of looked-after children."*[25]

Speaking after the judgment Mrs Johns said:

*"We are prepared to love and accept any child. All we were not willing to do was to tell a small child that the practice*

*of homosexuality was a good thing. We feel excluded and that there is no place for us in society."*[26]

The broader context for this case was a decision by all Catholic adoption agencies in the UK to close in 2010 as their view that a child should have both a mother and a father solely was now unlawful. The final Catholic adoption agency in the UK closed after the Charity Commissioners ruling in August of that year. In its ruling the Commission said:

*The Commission recognises that Catholic Care offers a valuable, high quality adoption service by providing assessment and preparation of people to act as adoptive parents for children being placed by local authorities. However, the Commission concluded that the evidence did not provide sufficiently convincing and weighty reasons to justify the charity's wish to restrict its service to heterosexual prospective adoptive parents.*[27]

## 8.7  NOT SO SPECIAL SUNDAY

In another case, it was held that Sunday was not protected as the Sabbath day for Christians. Ms. Mba is a practising Christian; she is a Sabbatarian who holds to the Biblical belief that no work should be undertaken on a Sunday. She has never worked a Sunday in her working life. Ms. Mba was constructively dismissed by her employer for refusing to work on a Sunday; the loss of livelihood is the most severe penalty that can be sustained for seeking to passively exercise one's religious beliefs. She has a minority belief within the Christian community.

Ms. Mba was an employee of the London Borough of Merton ("Merton LBC"). She was employed from 30th July 2007 – 30th June 2010 as a Residential Care Worker. The London Borough of Merton is a London administrative Council serving a population of approximately 200,000,[28] with a budget of approximately £488 million.[29]  It employs 5,430 individuals, of which approximately 4161 are full time.

National law requires the establishment of *'Group Discrimination'* as required by the decision in *Eweida* (as discussed above); to satisfy the test, evidence is required of disparate impact on *persons*.[30]

Therefore, in Ms. Mba's case, evidence was required to demonstrate that Sunday was the Rest day of the Christian faith as required by the *Ten Commandments*. Bishop Nazir-Ali is one of the most senior and respected Churchmen in the United Kingdom.  He was Bishop of Rochester from 1994-2009 with an accompanying seat in the House of Lords. The Bishop gave a short and concise Witness Statement[31] on the issue of Sunday as a Sabbath day for Christians, but stated in the final paragraph:

*Some Christians will not work on the Sabbath (except for mercies); others may work only on an emergency; some Christians will want to wear a cross to manifest their faith, others will manifest their faith in some other way.  What is important is reasonable accommodation by employers of religious faith and practice.*

The *Employment Tribunal* twisted this Statement to mean the exact opposite of what the Bishop was saying, namely that some Christians *would work on a Sunday* and thus held at paragraph [88] (underlining added):

*As stated earlier, we need to weigh in the balance the discriminatory impact of the PCP [32] upon the Claimant. We accept that the PCP impacted upon her genuinely and deeply held religious belief and observance, as we have described above.  However in terms of the <u>degree of disadvantage</u> to her, we bear in mind the following in particular:*

*(i) Her belief that Sunday should be a day of rest and worship upon which no paid employment was*

203

*undertaken, whilst deeply held is not a <u>core component</u>*
*of the Christian faith (in the sense that the phrase is*
*used in Ladele, …*

This case illuminates the animus of the Tribunals and Courts to Christian practice; and it is solely Christian practice to which barriers are erected. First, the feigning of ignorance about the Christian faith such as not knowing the cross is a Christian symbol that is a significant symbol of faith, or that Sunday is the Sabbath day for Christians is absurd. Secondly, the need to have a Witness Statement from a former Bishop to assert the obvious fact that Sunday is the Sabbath day and finally to purposely twist that statement to its opposite meaning. The decision was reversed after the decision in the European Court in *Eweida* which is now considered.

## 8.8  THE TURN AROUND: 2013

By 2012, the Courts of the United Kingdom had held that the cross, the Sunday Sabbath[33] and a belief in marriage as between a man and a woman were unprotected beliefs of Christians. As one wit said to me: *it's only a matter of time before the Courts declare the Ten Commandments illegal.*

In delivering judgment in the case of *Eweida, Chaplin, Ladele and McFarlane v The United Kingdom*, the European Court held that:

*As enshrined in Article 9, freedom of thought, conscience and religion is one of the foundations of a "democratic society" within the meaning of the Convention. In its religious dimension it is one of the most vital elements that go to make up the identity of believers and their conception of life.*[34]

And in commenting directly on Ms Eweida's case the court stated in relation to her enforced suspension without pay:

*"that the refusal by British Airways between September 2006 and February 2007 to allow the applicant to remain in her post while visibly wearing a cross amounted to an interference with her right to manifest her religion."* [35]

As stated earlier, this decision represented a significant shift in the application of the law of religious liberty in the United Kingdom. The first case to consider the impact of this decision on the effect of Article 9 in our domestic legal system was the appeal of *Mba v Merton London Borough Council*.[36] The Court of Appeal (Vos and Elias LJJ.) recognised that Article 9 should apply to application of national employment law and that the Employment Tribunal and Employment Appeal Tribunal had made an 'error of law'. Regrettably, they did not reverse the findings of fact (as opposed to the law) so the case is currently before the European Court of Human Rights.

## 8.9 RELIGIOUS FREE SPEECH:
## COMPOSITING ARTICLES 9 AND 10
## CORE ISSUES TRUST v TRANSPORT FOR LONDON

### *Overd and Stephenson*

There has followed from this decision of *Eweida* some interesting free speech cases in relation to religious speech. In 2012, prior to judgment of the European Court, the case of *Hammond* (as discussed above) has been to a significant degree reversed in the cases of *R v Overd* and *R v Stephenson*.

In the case of *Overd*, Michael Overd was a street preacher in Taunton who regularly quotes from the Bible. On one occasion he read from 1 Corinthians 6:9-12 which reads:

*Or do you not know that the unrighteous will not inherit the kingdom of God? Do not be deceived: neither the sexually immoral, nor idolaters, nor adulterers, nor men who practice homosexuality,[10] nor thieves, nor the greedy, nor drunkards, nor revilers, nor swindlers will inherit the kingdom of God.[11] And such were some of you. But you were washed, you were sanctified, you were justified in the name of the Lord Jesus Christ and by the Spirit of our God.*

As happens in such cases, the very moment he was reading this verse, a same sex couple in a civil partnership walked past him and they felt that these comments were directed against them and reported the matter to the Police.

In the case of *Stephenson*, a protest group called 'Abort 67' stood outside an abortion clinic in Brighton with graphic but accurate pictures of aborted foetuses. This was clearly upsetting to the many young women entering the clinic but it was a political protest that was no less shocking than many anti war demonstrations, or anti animal experimentation stalls in the market square.

Both Overd and Stephenson were charged under the Public Order Act 1986; and both were acquitted and rightly so. However, free speech is very limited in a democratic society if it is limited to the street protester or street preacher. This does not engage with the wider public. Thus, it is necessary to consider the right of Christians to place controversial messages that engage a wider public readership such as posters, advertising or the audio visual media.

### Core Issues v Transport for London

In *Core Issues Trust v Transport for London (TfL)*, an issue arose whether a poster campaign could be mounted that challenged the viewpoint of Stonewall on the controversial issue of homosexuality. Core Issues Trust ('CIT') is a religious organisation, and is a recognised Christian charity with the Charities Commission; it has a religious objective of promoting Christian values and lifestyle, and it is directed by Dr. Michael Davidson, who is an Ordained Minister. It is based in Northern Ireland.

CIT works with men and women who voluntarily seek assistance to move away from homosexual practice and feelings, where possible and appropriate. The charity is educative in practice, aiming to offer balanced information with both peer and professionally supported assistance where this is necessary and possible.

Article four of the Objects of Core Issues Trust, a company limited by guarantee (no.NI606015), upon which the group was incorporated, upholds the view that states:

*(4) ... that any sexual relationship outside marriage is inconsistent with the Biblical view of "one flesh" relationships (Genesis 2.24), and the Divine pattern for family life, premised on marriage between one man and one woman and to support those who seek to live according to that pattern.*

The charity's Statement of Belief includes the statement:

*that the Church of Jesus Christ, when true to the Scriptures, properly provides a spiritual home and sensitive support for believers and seekers who struggle with issues of sexual brokenness, including homosexuality.*

In 2012, Stonewall commenced a poster campaign entitled: *'Some People are Gay. Get over it'*. In response to this advertisement, the Claimants' proposed poster was: *'Not Gay!, Ex-Gay, Post- Gay and Proud. Get over it'*. The Applicants wanted a debate and differing dialogue over the issue of homosexuality and Christian mission.

The Mayor of London, Boris Johnson, was in a very close re-election campaign with Mr Livingstone. The poster was prevented from running. Transport for London held[37] that the poster placed by Core Issues Trust should be banned because:

- *the advertisement is likely to cause widespread or serious offense to members of the public on account of the nature of the product or service being advertised….*

- *the advertisement contains images or messages which relate to matters of public controversy and sensitivity*

The Mayor made significant political capital, publicly stating that he used his executive power to ban the CIT poster. Mayor Johnson defeated his rival Mr Livingstone by a mere 3%. There was considerable media comment at the time when the Mayor banned the poster. Some of the media comments were:

*"Mr Johnson used his powers as chairman of Transport for London to instruct the body to ditch the campaign. He said yesterday: 'London is one of the most tolerant cities in the world and intolerant of intolerance. It is clearly offensive to suggest that being gay is an illness that someone recovers from and I am not prepared to have that suggestion driven around London on our buses.'"*

(http://www.dailymail.co.uk/news/article-2128936/Gay-cure-advert-banned-London-buses-Boris-Johnson-TfL.html#axzz2KJUddFx7)

*He said that he made his decision not only because he thought an advert which suggested that gay people could be cured was likely to cause "great offence", but also because of the possible reverberations for London's Christian community. "The job of mayor is to unite, the job is to stop prejudice, and actually the backlash would be so intense it would not have been in the interest of Christian people in this city," he said.*

(http://www.guardian.co.uk/politics/2012/apr/19/boris-johnson-defends-advert-ban)

*The Evening Standard said he told the audience: "The job of mayor is to unite, to stop prejudice.*

*"The backlash would be so intense it would not have been in the interest of Christian people in this city." Ken Livingstone agreed with Mr Johnson's decision to pull the adverts, saying: "In my view Boris was right to pull them".*
(http://www.pinknews.co.uk/2012/04/19/boris-johnson-intense-backlash-against-ex-gay-bus-ads-would-have-hurt-christians/)

In the High Court hearing of the case, the learned judge held that both the Core Issues Trust poster *and* the Stonewall poster breached the *Advertising Policy of Transport for London*, but Lang J. went on to say ominously:

*But if the motive for the decision was to advance Mr Johnson's election campaign, at the expense of the proper exercise of TfL's powers and duties, this would call into question the lawfulness of the decision.*

Lang J. held in another part of the judgment on the question of free speech:

*[99]These observations echo the arguments in favour of free speech by the celebrated philosopher J.S. Mill (On Liberty, 1859) and more recently, the late Ronald Dworkin in the foreword to Extreme Speech and Democracy ed. Hare and Weinstein (2009), cited to me by Mr Diamond. Dworkin also warned against censorship on anti-discrimination grounds, saying:*

*"The strong conviction that freedom of speech is a universal value is challenged today not only by freedom's oldest opponents (the despots and ruling thieves who fear it), but also by new enemies who claim to speak for justice not tyranny. These new enemies point to other values we respect, including self-determination, equality, and freedom from racial hatred and prejudice, as reasons why the right of free speech should now be demoted to a much lower grade*

*of urgency and importance."*

*"These calls for censorship will strike many people as reasonable and signal, just for that reason, a new and particularly dangerous threat to free speech, for we are more likely to relax our defence of that freedom when our betrayers are foreign, or when the speech in question seems worthless or even vile. But if we do, then the principle is inevitably weakened, not just in such cases, but generally."*

### The Missing Evidence of the Mayor of London

Dr Mike Davidson pursued the issue of the *'missing evidence'* and made a 'Freedom of Information' request. By reply dated 24th April 2013 the Greater London Authority (GLA) forwarded an email which read:

*Boris has just instructed tfl to pull the adverts. And I have briefed the Guardian. Who will break that news in the next half hour.*

This email appeared to contradict the evidence given before Lang J., and the stage was set for an historic hearing before the Court of Appeal which gave an historic judgment on 27th January 2014 which held as follows:

- The Mayor should face an inquiry as to whether he used his powers for the *improper purpose* of advancing his re-election campaign [44] – [48];
- The Public Sector Equality Duty ('PSED') was applied in error by the learned Judge (Mrs Justice Lang). Whilst it was not a material error on the facts of this case, this holding was of considerable importance to all public authorities in relation to freedom of expression as the duty to equality did not mandate restrictions of freedom of speech [71]-[76];
- The Mayor had breached the terms of the Judgment of Lang J. by re-commencing the Stonewall campaign in October 2013 [80];

- Ex-gays were not *'regarded as a separate category of sexual orientation'*; however, such persons were protected by the *Equality Act 2010* [95]-[98]; this finding was of crucial importance to the Applicants as they were now able to use anti-discrimination legislation to prevent animus to their status;
- The learned Judge's original holding that the Core Issues Trust, Stonewall and British Humanist Association posters had all breached the Advertising Policy of Transport for London was upheld. The Claimant/Appellant formally/ technically failed in their Application for Judicial Review [83]-[89] and [103] simply because their poster was not permitted even though a level playing field was achieved;
- Lord Justice Briggs upheld the sensibilities of the Christian community in a separate speech: [104] – [105]; and it is worth repeating his words:

*[104] In my judgment she was also right to do so. There are many people, of many different faiths and none, who have been brought up and taught to believe that all homosexual conduct is wrong. Many have, after long and careful thought, arrived at a different view. Some have been encouraged along the way by bold expressions of the type found in the Stonewall advertisement. But many others continue sincerely to hold that belief, and some regard a departure from it as inconsistent with the maintenance of their faith. Some would rather give up their jobs, or discontinue their businesses, than act in a way which they believe condones such conduct, whether by conducting civil partnership or gay marriage ceremonies, by admitting gay couples to bed and breakfast accommodation, or by providing adoption training to gay couples. Sincere differences of view about this issue are tearing apart some religious communities, both here and abroad.*

*[105] Like my Lord, I consider that the Stonewall advertisement was probably intended to promote tolerance of gay people and to discourage homophobic bullying, and that this is plainly a lawful aim. But the advice to 'get over it' is a confrontational message which is likely to come across to many of those to whom I have just referred as at least disrespectful of their sincerely held beliefs, and to some as suggesting that there is no place for the toleration of their beliefs in modern society. Displayed on the side of London buses it is therefore likely to cause widespread offence to many, even if it may have promoted tolerance and understanding in others.*

The comments of Briggs LJ. are extremely positive words and represents the 'turn around' that has been achieved by the complete strategising of cases before the courts. At the time of writing in February 2015 the case continues before the European Court of Human Rights, and before the Court of Appeal in relation to the inquiry mentioned above.

8.10  CONCLUSION

There appears to be a unique hostility to the faith of Christians and that is why so many of these cases attract controversial publicity.

In: *Muir v Penisarwaun Care Home*,[38] there was no religious discrimination in repeatedly using Christian swear words in front of a Christian; in *Reaney v Hereford Diocesan Board of Finance*,[39] the Bishop of Hereford acted unreasonably in not appointing a homosexual as Youth Worker; in *Cherfi v G45 Security Services Ltd*[40] a Muslim who wanted to attend the (radical) Finsbury Park Mosque lost his case but shows the extent to which the employer went to accommodate him; in *Noah v The Wedge Hairdresser*,[41] a trendy hairdresser was held culpable for failing to employ a Muslim in a hijab (which was contrary to the image of the establishment) and even though no job existed; in *SG (by his litigation Friend) v Head Teacher & Governors of St. Gregory's Catholic Science College*[42] the High Court found that a school boy had been indirectly discriminated against on cultural grounds despite the fact that '*those who regard* [wearing their hair in corn rows] *as an obligation rather than a preference are in a minority': paragraph [32]* (contrast with *Mba*); and in *R (Watkins- Singh) v Governing Body of Aberdare Girls High School,*[43] there was both religious and racial discrimination for refusing to permit a Sikh schoolgirl to wear the Kara bracelet (which can be directly contrasted with *R (Playfoot) v Governing Body of Millais School*[44] where Christian schoolgirls failed to establish their right to wear *purity rings*[45]). And there are more examples.

In *Preddy v Bull,*[46] two Christian bed & breakfast owners lost their case on the right to uphold their moral view on marriage between a man and a woman. They were found to be discriminating against a same sex couple on two grounds. The first was that civil partnership was equivalent in law to marriage (now there is same sex marriage, this argument could not be run at all[47]) and secondly, the discrimination was against a core component of identity (sexual orientation).

Baroness Hale held:

*[38] Regard can also be had to the purpose of the Regulations, not as an aid to construction but in order to understand the problems they were meant to solve and how they proposed to solve them. The purpose was to secure that people of homosexual orientation were treated equally with people of heterosexual orientation by those in the business of supplying goods, facilities and services. Parliament was very well aware that there were deeply held religious objections to what was being proposed and careful consideration had been given to how best to accommodate these within the overall purpose...*

*[52] Sexual orientation is a core component of a person's identity which requires fulfilment through relationships with others of the same orientation. As Justice Sachs of the South African Constitutional Court movingly put it in National Coalition for Gay and Lesbian Equality v Minister of Justice, 1999 (1) SA 6, para 117:*

*"While recognising the unique worth of each person, the Constitution does not presuppose that a holder of rights is an isolated, lonely and abstract figure possessing a disembodied and socially disconnected self. It acknowledges that people live in their bodies, their communities, their cultures, their places and their times. The expression of sexuality requires a partner, real or imagined."*

*[53] Heterosexuals have known this about themselves and been able to fulfil themselves in this way throughout history. Homosexuals have also known this about themselves but were long denied the possibility of fulfilling themselves through relationships with others. This was an affront to their dignity as human beings which our law has now (some would say belatedly) recognised. Homosexuals can enjoy the same freedom and the same relationships as any others. But we should not underestimate the continuing legacy of those centuries of discrimination, persecution even, which is still going on in many parts of the world. It is no doubt for that reason that Strasbourg requires "very weighty reasons" to justify discrimination on grounds of sexual orientation. It is for that reason that we should be slow to accept that prohibiting hotel keepers from discriminating against homosexuals is a disproportionate limitation on their right to manifest their religion.*

The law of religious liberty is a fascinating, controversial and complex field of law. The issues relate directly to morality and accordingly attract wide interest. They also raise issues of individual freedom which are fundamental for the wellbeing of our society today.

*Endnotes*

[1] *Eweida & Others v United Kingdom:* Article 35 of the European Convention on Human Rights and Fundamental Freedoms (1950) implements the requirement of international law that before the Court can consider an Application, the Applicant must have exhausted all domestic remedies. The precise meaning of this requirement has been subject to interpretation by the Court. The full list of cases before the European Court of Human Rights was *Eweida* and *Chaplin* (on the right to wear a cross) and *Ladele* and *McFarlane* (on the right to a conscience exemption for Christians in the provision of services to same sex couples).

[2] The Auld Report (1984) HMSO by Auld J (as he was then).

[3] Article 30 of the EEC Treaty; now Article 28 on the *Treaty on the Functioning of the European Union: see Case 145/88 Torfean BC v B&Q plc and Case 169/91 Stoke City Council & Norwich City Council v B&Q plc*.

[4] *Case 120/78* the *'Cassis de Dijon'* case.

[5] The United Kingdom is a dualist system and international treaties require incorporation by means of an Act of Parliament. The United Kingdom was until 1998 the only modern democracy with neither a Constitution nor a Bill of Rights. The unwritten constitution was a slowly evolving political entity guided by the doctrine of the sovereignty of Parliament.

[6] 1926-2002. Baroness Young was the only woman appointed to the cabinet by Margaret Thatcher and was leader of the House of Lords 1981-3. I would describe her as formidable, brilliant and engaging; I can only imagine a cabinet with these two ladies in power.

[7] A monist State automatically incorporates international law, in some countries giving international law primacy over domestic legislation.

[8] http://www.legislation.gov.uk/ukpga/1986/64

[9] http://www.bailii.org/cgi-bin/markup.cgi?doc=/ew/cases/EWHC/Admin/2004/69.html

[10] [2004] EWHC 69 (Admin)

[11] http://ukcommentators.blogspot.co.uk/2004/10/harry-hammond-day.html

[12] A form of Hindu 'ponytail' that is worn by some men.

[13] The Star of David was additionally banned.

[14] From Ms Eweida's viewpoint.

[15] The case continued as *British Airways* argued this was a concession, they had acted within the law and Ms Eweida was not entitled to damages for loss of income during her suspension.

[16] See in particular Lord Bingham's comments in *R (Begum) v Headteachers and Governors of Debigh High School* at paragraph [23]. In this case a Muslim girl wanted to wear the *Jilbab* which was resisted by the school.

[17] *R (SB) v Governors of Denbigh High School* [2006] UKHL 15, at paragraph [23].

[18] Paragraph [37] of Judgment.

[19] Eweida v British Airways [2012] in the Court of Appeal at paragraphs [25] and [40].

[20] She has argued that Muslim staff were permitted to wear an approved Hijab; and she was required to remove her Cross that she had always worn for the last 30 years.

[21] [2013]

[22] [2010]

[23] All decisions of the Court of Appeal are binding on other Courts of Appeal and all lower courts.

[24] [2011]

[25] http://www.bailii.org/ew/cases/EWHC/Admin/2011/375.html

[26] http://www.telegraph.co.uk/news/religion/8353538/Foster-parent-ban-we-have-not-received-justice.html

[27] http://www.charitycommission.gov.uk/RSS/News/pr_catholic_care.aspx

[28] 199,700 on 2011 ONS census estimate.

[29] Summary of Accounts for year 2013/14. Approximately £178 million are spent on services.

[30] Now Section 19 of the Equality Act 2010.

[31] Annexed to this Application.

[32] Practice, Criteria or Provision: PCP in cases of indirect discrimination.

[33] Mba v Merton London Borough Council (2012) Employment Tribunal

[34] http://hudoc.echr.coe.int/sites/eng/pages/search.aspx?i=001-115881

[35] ibid

[36] [2014] ICR 357, CA

[37] Letter dated 4th July 2012.

[38] Case No. 1600651/2013 of 18th June 2014.

[39] Case No. 1602844/2006

[40] Case No. UKEAT/0379/10/DM

[41] Case No. 2201867/2007 of 11th June 2008.

[42] [2010]

[43] [2008] EWHC 1865 (Admin)

[44] [2007] ELR 484

[45] A practice in which young Christians wear a ring as a symbol of their commitment to remain chaste until marriage.

[46] [2013] 1 WLR 3741

[47] Marriage (Same Sex) Act 2013.